Inner Bonding Daily
INSPIRATIONS

Inner Bonding Daily
INSPIRATIONS

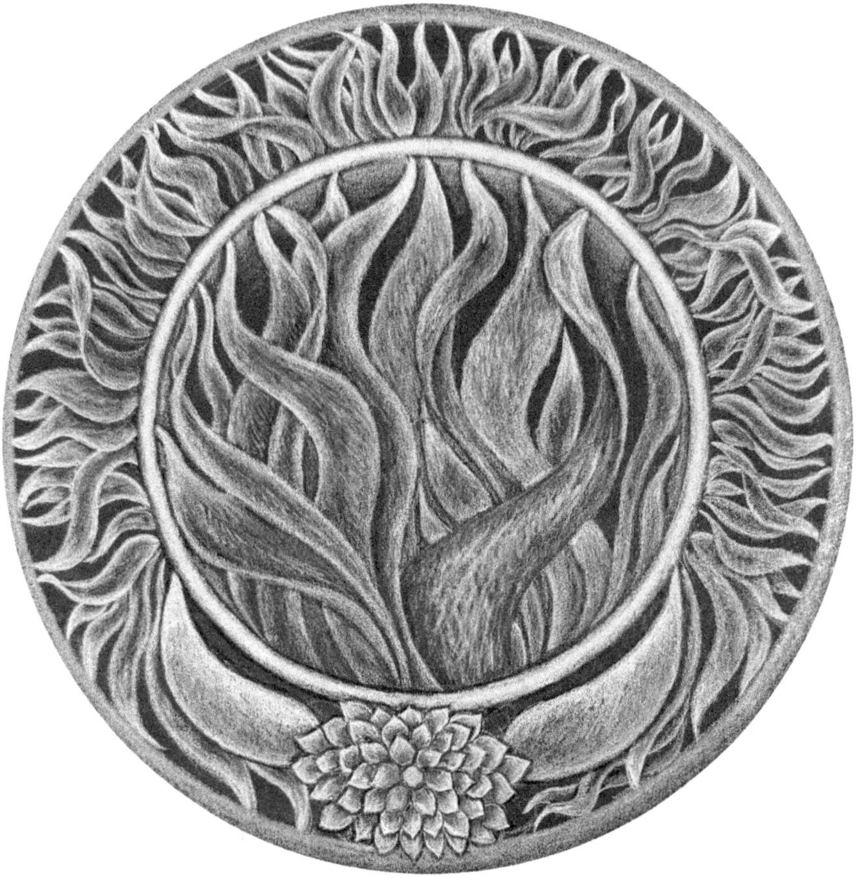

Margaret Paul, PhD

MEDIA

Published 2024 by Gildan Media LLC
aka G&D Media
www.GandDmedia.com

INNER BONDING DAILY INSPIRATIONS. Copyright © 2024 Margaret Paul, PhD. All rights reserved.

No part of this book may be reproduced or transmitted in any form, by any means, (electronic, photocopying, recording, or otherwise) without the prior written permission of the author. No liability is assumed with respect to the use of the information contained within. Although every precaution has been taken, the author and publisher assume no liability for errors or omissions. Neither is any liability assumed for damages resulting from the use of the information contained herein.

Interior design by Meghan Day Healey of Story Horse, LLC.

Library of Congress Cataloging-in-Publication Data is available upon request

ISBN: 978-1-7225-0709-1

10   9   8   7   6   5   4   3   2   1

Inner Bonding Daily
INSPIRATIONS

January 1

We all want to find our tribe, the people we resonate with, our true family. We are not meant to be alone, but our family of origin may not be our true family. Open to the possibility of coming home to your true family, your family of choice, the people who love and support you.

Journaling
Reflections on the Daily Inspiration

_____
_____
_____
_____
_____
_____
_____

January 2

Are you looking outside or inside for the source of your anxiety? If you are feeling anything other than peace, look within at your own thoughts and beliefs for the source of anxiety, depression, guilt, or shame.

Journaling
Reflections on the Daily Inspiration

___
___
___
___
___
___
___

January 3

Creating the habit of thinking about love, and about what is love to yourself and others, will keep you connected with spirit. When you are with spirit, you will not be in fear.

Journaling
Reflections on the Daily Inspiration

_____
_____
_____
_____
_____
_____
_____

January 4

We cannot get to know each other just through talking. We get to know each other deeply through being—laughing, crying, playing, loving, fighting, making up. Words are easy—anyone can say anything about themselves. But we cannot hide our intent in our real interactions. We cannot know someone's heart through words alone.

Journaling
Reflections on the Daily Inspiration

_____
_____
_____
_____
_____
_____
_____

January 5

True compassion starts with oneself. If you extend compassion to others before giving it to yourself, you are giving from an empty place and your compassion may be manipulative. But if you give it to yourself and then extend it to others, you are giving from a full place within. Then your compassion is truly loving and healing because you don't need anything back.

Journaling
Reflections on the Daily Inspiration

___
___
___
___
___
___
___

January 6

Creativity enlivens the being. All of us are born with different creative gifts, but many of us have not manifested these gifts. Today, notice how your essence wants to express your creativity—through music, art, writing, or movement?

Journaling
Reflections on the Daily Inspiration

_____
_____
_____
_____
_____
_____
_____

January 7

Do you allow yourself to dump your negative energy onto others? Just as we do not go around stabbing others with a knife, we need to not be stabbing others with our negative energy—our anger, fear, anxiety, and stress. It's appropriate to share it if we want help, but dumping it is an avoidance of personal responsibility. Today, notice your energy around others.

Journaling
Reflections on the Daily Inspiration

January 8

Attend to the difference between love and approval. Approval comes and goes, while love is constant. We can manipulate approval by doing things "right" but love from others is always a free gift that is beyond our control. We convince ourselves that we can have control over getting love, but are you sure this is true?

Journaling
Reflections on the Daily Inspiration

___
___
___
___
___
___
___

January 9

Spirit energizes us when we pursue that which we are passionate about. Are you passionate about your work, your hobbies, your volunteer activities, your home and family, your pets, your health and well-being, your relationship with spirit? Find your passion and sense of meaning and you will find your joy and aliveness.

Journaling
Reflections on the Daily Inspiration

_____
_____
_____
_____
_____
_____
_____

January 10

Do you expect to feel the feeling of love before taking the actions of love? Try taking the actions of love first. You might notice that acting loving leads to feeling loving!

Journaling
Reflections on the Daily Inspiration

___
___
___
___
___
___
___

January 11

Spirit is light. The more we embrace our own lightness of being, the more we will feel and hear the guidance of spirit. Today, stay in lightness of being by following your joy and expressing gratitude for this sacred journey of evolving your soul in love.

Journaling
Reflections on the Daily Inspiration

_____
_____
_____
_____
_____
_____
_____

January 12

The moment you awaken each morning, move into gratitude for the sacred privilege of being on this soul's journey. There are some soul lessons we can only experience by being here in a body on this planet. Remembering to embrace this journey with gratitude throughout the day will make the journey a joy.

Journaling
Reflections on the Daily Inspiration

___
___
___
___
___
___

January 13

When you meet someone or see a friend or family member, do you offer your smile and your welcome, or do you wait for them to reach out first? Today, don't wait!

Journaling
Reflections on the Daily Inspiration

___
___
___
___
___
___
___
___

January 14

Heartache, heartbreak, or loneliness—which we likely feel whenever someone is mean, closed, rejecting, threatening, or blaming—are the core feelings most people avoid feeling with their various addictions. Today, instead of avoiding these feelings, acknowledge them and embrace them with deep compassion. This is what allows them to move through you rather than getting stuck in you.

Journaling
Reflections on the Daily Inspiration

January 15

How often do you argue, defend, explain, threaten, attack, or blame rather than feel the authentic heartache of another's unloving behavior? This week, practice attending to your heartache with deep compassion rather than avoiding this feeling with controlling behavior.

Journaling
Reflections on the Daily Inspiration

_____
_____
_____
_____
_____
_____
_____

January 16

Today, notice which you focus on more—what brings you joy or what causes fear. Notice that it is often your own thoughts and actions that create either joy or fear. Becoming aware of which you are choosing in any given moment gives you the power to change your thoughts and actions and take responsibility for your feelings.

Journaling
Reflections on the Daily Inspiration

January 17

Free will is a great gift. Because of free will, we have the opportunity to choose who we want to be each moment. We can also choose to be unconscious of this choice. Today, be conscious of choosing who you want to be—loving or unloving, open or closed, in surrender to spirit or attempting to control, learning about love or protected against pain.

Journaling
Reflections on the Daily Inspiration

_____
_____
_____
_____
_____
_____
_____

January 18

Today, focus only on thinking thoughts and taking actions that create peace within. Today, let go of attempting to control anything outside of yourself and focus only on what you can control—your own thoughts and actions. Today, be willing to release to spirit all stressful feelings—anger, fear, anxiety, hurt. Today, make creating peace within your only goal.

Journaling
Reflections on the Daily Inspiration

___
___
___
___
___
___

January 19

Let joy be your guide. Our joy is how God lets us know we are being loving to ourselves. What fills your heart and brings you joy?

Journaling
Reflections on the Daily Inspiration

January 20

Act as if you are not alone. Act as if you are being held and guided by your guidance each moment of the day. Notice how you feel when you act as if you are not alone.

Journaling
Reflections on the Daily Inspiration

___
___
___
___
___
___
___

January 21

When you are with another person, if your focus is primarily on what they want and feel, you may be trying to control how they feel about you. Today, attend to taking responsibility for what you want and how you feel.

Journaling
Reflections on the Daily Inspiration

___
___
___
___
___
___
___

January 22

Do you have a dream? Are you following your dream? Are you spending time each day manifesting your dream? Life has aliveness when you have the courage to follow your dreams.

Journaling
Reflections on the Daily Inspiration

_____
_____
_____
_____
_____
_____
_____
_____

January 23

Remember that your feelings are informing you of whether you are on track or off track in your thinking and behavior. Remember to notice your feelings throughout the day.

Journaling
Reflections on the Daily Inspiration

_____
_____
_____
_____
_____
_____
_____

January 24

Today, think about what you do that makes you feel invisible to others. Do you give in to others rather than stand in your truth? Do you avoid asking for what you want to avoid rejection? Do you act like everything is okay when it isn't? Do you agree with others to avoid conflict? Do you ignore your own feelings but attend to other's feelings? Today notice how you might be making yourself invisible.

Journaling
Reflections on the Daily Inspiration

_____
_____
_____
_____
_____
_____
_____

January 25

Set your intentions for the day. Make a conscious decision that you want to be in compassion, love, peace, and joy. Decide to be courageous and speak your truth. Request to draw to you all that is of the light, and to be immune to the darkness of anger, fear, and judgment.

Journaling
Reflections on the Daily Inspiration

___
___
___
___
___
___
___

January 26

Today, choose to be non-reactive in situations that normally push your buttons. Choose to remain silent rather than argue your point. Choose to listen rather than interrupt. Choose to accept rather than judge. Choose to tell your truth rather than be invisible. Choose to care about another rather than resist being controlled. Choose to learn rather than protect when your buttons are pushed.

Journaling
Reflections on the Daily Inspiration

January 27

Who do you want to be today? You get to choose each moment to be loving or unloving, open or closed, controlling or in surrender to spirit, protected or learning. Each moment, notice the choice you are making.

Journaling
Reflections on the Daily Inspiration

January 28

Don't ever forget the magic of life—the beauty of flowers and trees and fluffy white clouds. Don't forget the magic of babies and puppies and kittens. Don't forget the magic of kindness, compassion, and the sharing of love. It's the magic and beauty of life that makes it all worthwhile.

Journaling
Reflections on the Daily Inspiration

January 29

Truth, love, peace, and joy are all words that describe God and are synonymous with God. To be loving, peaceful and joyful, we need to be in truth, which means that we need to accept the reality of what we can control and what we can't. Today, focus on opening to learning about truth.

Journaling
Reflections on the Daily Inspiration

___
___
___
___
___
___
___

January 30

Today, think about what brings you joy to give to those you care about and those you love—and then give it!

Journaling
Reflections on the Daily Inspiration

_____
_____
_____
_____
_____
_____
_____

January 31

Did you feel seen by your parents? Did they see you as a good person? Do you feel seen by the people in your life now? How often do you explain or defend yourself, hoping to control how someone sees you? Today, notice the things you do to attempt to control how others see you. You might be doing this to avoid the loneliness of not being seen, yet embracing the loneliness and seeing yourself lightens the being.

Journaling
Reflections on the Daily Inspiration

___
___
___
___
___
___
___

February 1

We all want connection with others. Without connection we may feel lonely. Yet the most important connection is with our own feelings and our higher guidance. Without this connection, we feel alone. Today, be conscious of staying connected with yourself instead of just focusing on connecting with others.

Journaling
Reflections on the Daily Inspiration

February 2

Do you play enough? Do you have creative time? Do you have enough fun? Do you have enough laughter in your life? Do you get enough rest? Do you get done the things you need to get done? Today, focus on creating balance in your life between work and play, between doing and being, between time with others and time alone.

Journaling
Reflections on the Daily Inspiration

_____
_____
_____
_____
_____
_____
_____

February 3

Your ego—your wounded self—is a child or adolescent who is acting out in ways that are harmful for you. Your job as a loving adult is to love but not to indulge this wounded child. Your job is to set solid limits on what you think, how you act, what you put into your body, what you say to others. If you want to stay in peace and joy, you cannot indulge your wounded self.

Journaling
Reflections on the Daily Inspiration

___
___
___
___
___
___
___

February 4

What are you grateful for today? Notice the everyday things—food, water, your hands, your feet, your eyes to see, you ears to hear. Notice the flowers, the trees, the birds, the animals. Notice your ability to be kind, to help others. Today, express your gratitude for the everyday things in your life, and for your life itself—this miraculous journey of the soul.

Journaling
Reflections on the Daily Inspiration

February 5

Do you judge others or accept others? Do you judge yourself or accept yourself? Today, notice who you choose to be, accepting or judgmental. Who you choose to be has nothing to do with who someone else is or what they are doing. You have free will to choose to be loving or unloving, accepting or judgmental. No one determines that for you, no matter what they are doing.

Journaling
Reflections on the Daily Inspiration

_____
_____
_____
_____
_____
_____
_____

February 6

When conflict occurs, you will learn the most if you take 100% responsibility for the conflict. Worrying about the other person's part of the conflict will get you nowhere, other than feeling like a victim. By taking 100% responsibility for the conflict, you empower yourself to see what you are doing that is not in your highest good and change it.

Journaling
Reflections on the Daily Inspiration

___
___
___
___
___
___

February 7

It takes courage to stand in your truth. It takes courage to speak your truth when you fear others may be angry, rejecting, punishing. Yet when you make controlling how others think of you more important than speaking your truth, you lose yourself, you lose your integrity. Today ask yourself which is more important—others' approval or your integrity.

Journaling
Reflections on the Daily Inspiration

_____
_____
_____
_____
_____
_____
_____

February 8

When you do not accept that which you cannot change, you will feel angry and frustrated. Today, notice the energy you spend in not accepting what you cannot change: your partner, traffic, the weather, rude people and so on. Focus on accepting what is and notice the peace you feel.

Journaling
Reflections on the Daily Inspiration

_____
_____
_____
_____
_____
_____
_____

February 9

Do you have an inner critical taskmaster who keeps telling you what to do? Do you have another inner part that resists being told what to do? Do you get stuck in procrastination due to this inner power struggle? Do you find that you automatically resist doing whatever someone else wants you to do? Today, notice your resistance and where it is coming from—within and/or without.

Journaling
Reflections on the Daily Inspiration

_____
_____
_____
_____
_____
_____
_____

February 10

Spirit offers us four incredible gifts: truth, love, peace, and joy. When you open to the gifts of spirit, you will always be guided toward your highest good—your truth, love, peace, and joy. You cannot experience these gifts without spirit, because they are spirit. Whenever you know truth, and feel peace, love, and joy, you are one with spirit.

Journaling
Reflections on the Daily Inspiration

_____
_____
_____
_____
_____
_____

February 11

The real challenge in staying conscious is to take loving action on your own behalf. As soon as you don't, it is likely you will feel numb or angry. The numbness is your inner child's way of not feeling the pain of the inner abandonment. The anger is your inner child's anger at you for the inner abandonment. Notice your numbness or anger and take the loving action.

Journaling
Reflections on the Daily Inspiration

___
___
___
___
___
___
___

February 12

Research indicates that happy people create happy relationships, not the other way around! If you believe you need a relationship to be happy or the "right" relationship, you may stay stuck being unhappy. Unhappy people either don't get into relationships, or often create unhappy relationships. Put your energy into making yourself happy and then see what happens!

Journaling
Reflections on the Daily Inspiration

___
___
___
___
___
___
___

February 13

Today, tune into the frequency of color. What colors resonate with your own being? What colors make you feel warm, cozy and at home? What colors feel like old friends, and what colors are dissonant with your frequency? Today, adorn yourself with friendly colors!

Journaling
Reflections on the Daily Inspiration

_____
_____
_____
_____
_____
_____
_____

February 14

Forgiveness is the natural outcome of doing your inner work. As you learn to embrace and heal your own wounded self with love, you see that others' unloving behavior toward you comes from a small, wounded child within them. Compassion for yourself and your woundedness leads to compassion for others and their woundedness. Forgiveness occurs naturally through your compassion for yourself and for others.

Journaling
Reflections on the Daily Inspiration

_____
_____
_____
_____
_____
_____

February 15

If people could read your mind, what would you not want them to know? Today, focus on thinking only thoughts that you would be happy to share with others. Today, think only thoughts that energize rather than deplete your being.

Journaling
Reflections on the Daily Inspiration

___
___
___
___
___
___

February 16

Your body is the house of your soul. How do you treat this house of your soul? Do you feed it pure food filled with life and energy? Do you exercise it and rest it enough? Do you adorn it in colors that feel good? Do you provide it with loving touch? Today, do all you can to love your body, the wonderful house of your soul.

Journaling
Reflections on the Daily Inspiration

_____
_____
_____
_____
_____
_____

February 17

Today, think of something you always wanted to do and have not yet done. Go inside to your inner child and remember a way you wanted to have fun or create or have adventure or remember something you wanted to learn to do. Today make plans to do it. It may take time to bring this about, but it is loving action and will bring you joy.

Journaling
Reflections on the Daily Inspiration

_____
_____
_____
_____
_____
_____
_____

February 18

The more you choose to be present in the moment, the more you will experience the love, peace, joy, and creativity of spirit. To be present in the moment, you must be willing to let go of control and surrender to being guided by spirit. Today "sit" on your wounded self—the part of you who wants control and allow the presence of love to move through you.

Journaling
Reflections on the Daily Inspiration

_____
_____
_____
_____
_____
_____
_____

February 19

Be mindful of your energy. The energy of every thought, every word, and every action, affects the whole of consciousness. Today, be conscious of pouring loving thoughts, actions, and words into the oneness of spirit.

Journaling
Reflections on the Daily Inspiration

February 20

Who is in charge in this moment—your loving adult or your wounded self? Are you connecting with spirit and bringing that love and truth within, or are you stuck in your mind trying to figure everything out? Challenge yourself to move beyond your mind and into love and truth.

Journaling
Reflections on the Daily Inspiration

February 21

True caring is not conditional. It is not based on what you get from someone, but on who you choose to be in the world. Caring comes from feeling your oneness with all living beings and choosing to support the highest good of all.

Journaling
Reflections on the Daily Inspiration

_____
_____
_____
_____
_____
_____
_____

February 22

When you spend time with someone, is your intent to give or to get? Notice in your interactions with others if you are sharing your caring and understanding, or if you are trying to get attention and approval. Or are you giving to get—giving caring to get approval? Noticing your intent can help you shift from trying to get to wanting to give and share.

Journaling
Reflections on the Daily Inspiration

_____
_____
_____
_____
_____
_____
_____

February 23

Courage is taking the loving action in the face of fear, rather than letting fear govern your choices. If there was no fear, there would be no need for courage. Therefore, fear is no reason to wait to take the loving action on your own behalf.

Journaling
Reflections on the Daily Inspiration

February 24

When someone is being unloving to you, do you believe that you can get them to be loving? Do you believe if you argue, lecture, convince, get angry, punish, withdraw your love—you can control their intent? Today, practice accepting your helplessness over others' feelings and behavior, and then take loving action in your own behalf.

Journaling
Reflections on the Daily Inspiration

_____
_____
_____
_____
_____
_____
_____

February 25

Notice how you treat others when you are tired, fearful, stressed, anxious, depressed. Do you take out on others your own inner struggles? Notice how you feel about yourself when you treat others unlovingly.

Journaling
Reflections on the Daily Inspiration

February 26

Noticing the beauty around you—the beauty of a flower, a tree, a plant, a child, a pet, a loved one—will bring you into the present moment. It is in this present moment that you can experience the beauty that you are and the love and truth of your source that is always present.

Journaling
Reflections on the Daily Inspiration

_____
_____
_____
_____
_____
_____
_____

February 27

Letting your inner child know that you are loved is one of the greatest gifts you can give to yourself. Today, be an emissary of God and allow the love that is God to manifest through you to your inner child. Take the actions of love for yourself!

Journaling
Reflections on the Daily Inspiration

_____
_____
_____
_____
_____
_____
_____

February 28

Today, allow the beauty of nature to connect you with the beauty of your own essence, your true self. Look into a flower and see your light. Touch a tree and feel your soul. View a mountain and embrace the truth of who you are.

Journaling
Reflections on the Daily Inspiration

_____
_____
_____
_____
_____
_____
_____

February 29

Setting your intention as soon as you wake up each morning is a powerful thing to do. Today, set your intent to be one with spirit, to walk in love, peace, joy, and freedom. Set your intent to draw to you all that is of the light and in your highest good, and to be immune to darkness.

Journaling
Reflections on the Daily Inspiration

___
___
___
___
___
___
___

March 1

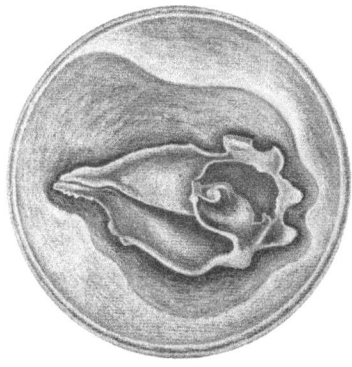

Open your heart to the beauty around you—to the wonder of nature, to the caring of others, to expressions of creativity, to the presence and joy of animals. Allow the beauty around you to open your heart to love.

Journaling
Reflections on the Daily Inspiration

___
___
___
___
___
___
___

March 2

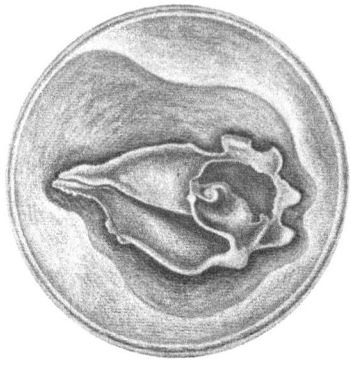

Our feelings of anger, fear, anxiety, hurt, depression, guilt, shame, and jealousy come from our thoughts. The feeling is the teacher—the indicator that our thoughts are off track. Ask for help from spirit in understanding what the thought/belief is behind the feeling. Then ask spirit for the truth.

Journaling
Reflections on the Daily Inspiration

March 3

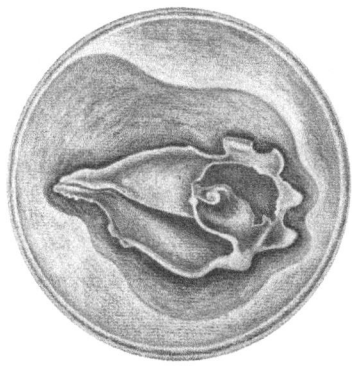

Today, notice your anger, irritation, or frustration. Notice that you may feel these feelings when you are not accepting your powerlessness over others and the outcome of things—when you want to control others and outcomes. Today, attempt to accept what is and then control what you can control—your own reactions.

Journaling
Reflections on the Daily Inspiration

___
___
___
___
___
___

March 4

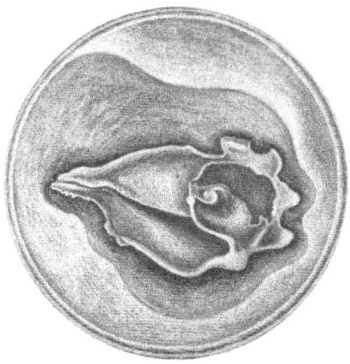

Our wounded self always wants to control our pain, others, and outcomes. If we judge ourselves for our controlling behavior, we become stuck in another level of control. The spiritual journey is about embracing our wounded selves with love and compassion rather than judgment, so we can learn about and let go of our controlling behavior.

Journaling
Reflections on the Daily Inspiration

_____
_____
_____
_____
_____
_____

March 5

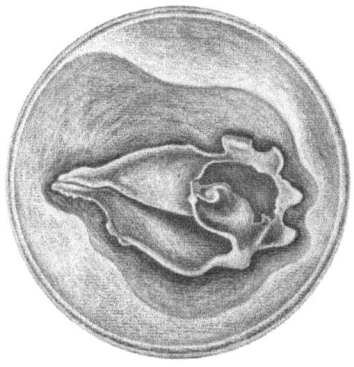

The wounded self never wants to give up control, believing it knows more than God. Today, notice who you are putting in charge—your wounded self or spirit. When you put your wounded self in charge, you will feel anxious and stressed. When you surrender to spirit being in charge, you will feel peace and joy.

Journaling
Reflections on the Daily Inspiration

March 6

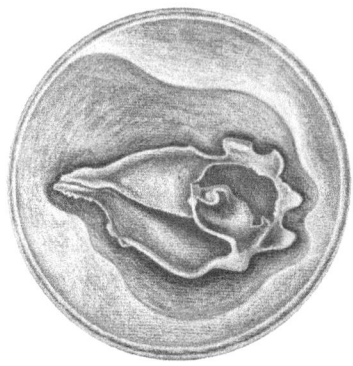

What journey are you on—earthly or spiritual? Is your journey motivated by love, starting with yourself, or is your journey motivated by getting love and avoiding pain? Are you doing to define your being, or are you doing to express your being? Do you give to others but not to yourself? Do you expect others or work or food or TV or alcohol or drugs to fill your emptiness instead of opening to spirit to fill you with love and peace? Today, notice, without judgment, the journey you are on, moment by moment.

Journaling
Reflections on the Daily Inspiration

_____
_____
_____
_____
_____
_____
_____

March 7

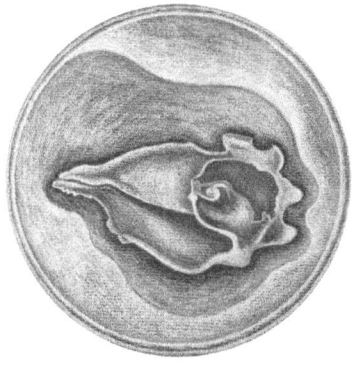

Do you feel unseen by others? Then you are not seeing yourself. Do you feel unheard by others? Then you are not hearing yourself. Do you feel discounted by others? Then you are not appreciating yourself. Today, focus on seeing, listening to, attending to, and appreciating yourself.

Journaling
Reflections on the Daily Inspiration

_____
_____
_____
_____
_____
_____
_____

March 8

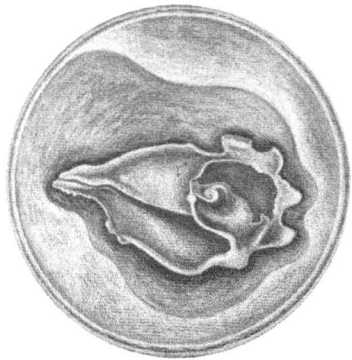

When you tune inside, do you feel empty or full? Emptiness is letting you know that your wounded self is in charge, and you are disconnected from the love that is spirit. When you open to learning about loving yourself—loving the beautiful essence that is the spark of God within—your heart opens to guidance and love fills your being. Today, stay tuned in to whether you feel empty or full inside.

Journaling
Reflections on the Daily Inspiration

_____
_____
_____
_____
_____
_____

March 9

Today, notice if you are speaking up for yourself, or if you are withdrawing, giving yourself up, or getting angry instead. Notice how great you feel when you take care of yourself as opposed to when you abandon yourself!

Journaling
Reflections on the Daily Inspiration

March 10

When someone does something we do not like and does not want to stop doing it, or someone won't do what we want, we have only two choices: we can accept them, or we can leave them. What we cannot do is get them to change. Yet trying to have control over getting others to change is where many people spend their energy.

Journaling
Reflections on the Daily Inspiration

March 11

Notice whether or not you are willing to lose yourself rather than risk losing others. Do you say yes to things you don't want to do in the hope of controlling how others feel about you? Do you compromise yourself in any way out of fear of disapproval? Notice how you feel when you are willing to lose yourself rather than risk losing others.

Journaling
Reflections on the Daily Inspiration

_____
_____
_____
_____
_____
_____
_____

March 12

Today, put two sticky notes wherever you are that say: "What am I trying to control or avoid?" "What is the loving action?" Whenever you feel any stress, ask these questions, and allow the answers to come from spirit.

Journaling
Reflections on the Daily Inspiration

___
___
___
___
___
___
___

March 13

Do you know who you are in your essence—the spark of the Divine within you? When you know and cherish your essence, you will never feel inadequate. Today, open to learning with your guidance about who you really are.

Journaling
Reflections on the Daily Inspiration

_____
_____
_____
_____
_____
_____
_____

March 14

Enlightenment means you have let go of the control of the wounded self and are fully present to and guided by spirit in this moment. Consciousness means that you are aware of when you are trying to control or are in surrender to spirit. Today attempt to be conscious of the wounded self's desire to control.

Journaling
Reflections on the Daily Inspiration

_____
_____
_____
_____
_____
_____

March 15

Anxiety and control are intricately linked. When our intent is to control that which we cannot control—others and outcomes—we will always feel anxious. Our anxiety is telling us that we are off base—that we need to take loving action for ourselves rather than continue to try to control others.

Journaling
Reflections on the Daily Inspiration

_____
_____
_____
_____
_____
_____
_____

March 16

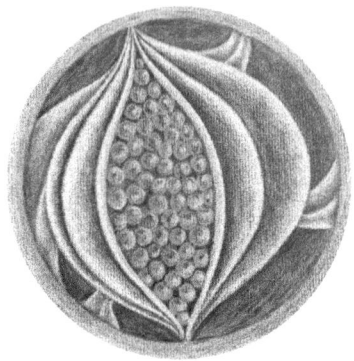

All distress comes from trying to control that which we cannot control. When you move out of the illusion of control and accept the reality of your lack of control over others and outcomes, then you are left with opening to your guidance and taking loving care of yourself. This is the key to inner peace and joy!

Journaling
Reflections on the Daily Inspiration

March 17

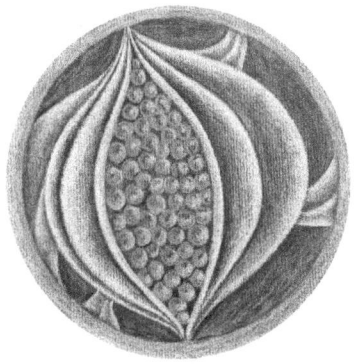

When we get beyond competition and comparison, we can then move into the great joy of being inspired by those further along than we are. Then you can experience a master at his or her work and be truly filled by the joy of experiencing mastery!

Journaling
Reflections on the Daily Inspiration

March 18

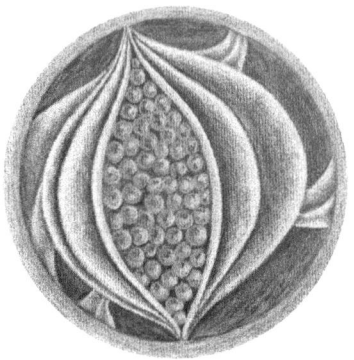

If you are not letting yourself do what brings you joy, attend to what you fear that is stopping you. Do you fear rejection or failure? Do you fear doing well and then losing your free time? Not following your joy and passion indicates that your loving adult is not creating a safe space for your essence to express itself. Today, notice the beliefs that are limiting you.

Journaling
Reflections on the Daily Inspiration

March 19

Do you daydream? Notice your intent when you are daydreaming. If your intent is to control, you will be daydreaming about events over which you have no control. These daydreams are attempts to control the outcome. These daydreams are a waste of energy. These daydreams indicate your lack of faith in spirit supporting your highest good. Positive daydreams are creative and point the way toward manifestation of your gifts.

Journaling
Reflections on the Daily Inspiration

_____
_____
_____
_____
_____
_____

March 20

Today, notice if you have balance—giving and receiving, between work and play, between doing and being. If you are not in balance, you are not being loving to yourself. Today, focus on creating balance in your life.

Journaling
Reflections on the Daily Inspiration

_____
_____
_____
_____
_____
_____
_____

March 21

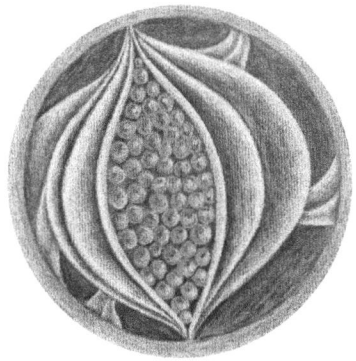

Just as you would not think to give a cigarette, an alcoholic drink, or a recreational drug to a crying child, consider not using substances to soothe your agitated inner child. An upset child, inner or outer, needs love, not pacifiers. You will learn what to do to soothe your feelings when you are ready to learn about what you may be doing to cause them and what your inner child needs from you to feel loved.

Journaling
Reflections on the Daily Inspiration

_____
_____
_____
_____
_____
_____
_____

March 22

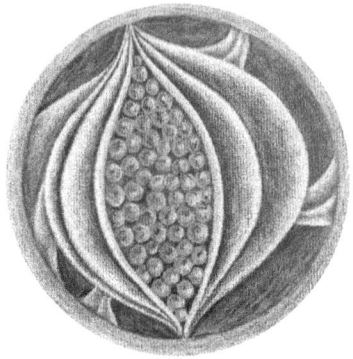

Today, the moment you feel anxious, depressed, hurt, or angry, notice how you did not take loving care of yourself in some situation. These feelings are always a communication from your inner guidance that you are abandoning yourself in some way.

Journaling
Reflections on the Daily Inspiration

_____
_____
_____
_____
_____
_____
_____

March 23

Sometimes everything has to be pulled out from under you before you finally let go of control and surrender to God, to spirit, to the unconditional love that is available to you. Sometimes things have to fall apart before we let go and let God. But it doesn't have to be that way.

Journaling
Reflections on the Daily Inspiration

_____
_____
_____
_____
_____
_____
_____

March 24

Today, spend some time in nature. Allow yourself to feel the beauty of nature in your body. Stand on dirt or grass and allow the power of Mother Earth to move through you, energizing you. Imagine nature spirits tending to the flowers and trees. Allow God to speak to you through nature.

Journaling
Reflections on the Daily Inspiration

March 25

Judging someone or disliking someone are not the same thing. When we judge someone, we are saying they are a good or bad person. We can dislike who a person chooses to be without judging them as good or bad. It is loving to ourselves to not be around people we dislike, but it is never loving to ourselves or others to be judgmental.

Journaling
Reflections on the Daily Inspiration

March 26

The challenge on the spiritual path is to reach such a deep place of inner security that we are able to stay open to learning with ourselves and with spirit, no matter what. This means being able to be loving to ourselves in the face of others attacking, blaming, crazy making, withdrawing. It means staying open to learning with spirit regarding our own highest good and the highest good of all, no matter what.

Journaling
Reflections on the Daily Inspiration

March 27

A sense of entitlement is common these days. People who feel entitled believe they are better than others, that they are more important than others, that their needs should come first. They are the takers. Caretakers support the takers. Caretakers believe they are not as important as others, that their needs should come last. Both takers and caretakers need to practice compassion for themselves and for others.

Journaling
Reflections on the Daily Inspiration

___
___
___
___
___
___

March 28

Are your background subtle thoughts about complains or about gratitude? Start to notice your background thoughts, as these subtle thoughts are a part of what determines whether you are feeling anxious or depressed, or filled with peace and joy. You cannot manifest what you want when you are complaining about your life, but you can when you consciously feel and express gratitude in the moment.

Journaling
Reflections on the Daily Inspiration

___
___
___
___
___
___
___

March 29

Why waste any energy on changing what you cannot change—others and outcomes. Better to spend your energy changing what you can change, which is you—your intent. Your experience of others and outcomes will change when you become who you came here to become—a loving, giving, peaceful, joyful, and creative human being.

Journaling
Reflections on the Daily Inspiration

_____
_____
_____
_____
_____
_____
_____

March 30

When someone who cares about you tells you that you are not open—that your energy is difficult, believe them. Others perceive our intention far more clearly than we do. It is a great gift when someone has the courage to tell us the truth, so accept it as a gift rather than a criticism and learn from it rather than deny or resist it.

Journaling
Reflections on the Daily Inspiration

March 31

Love has no conditions upon which it is withdrawn. It is steadfast, even when we do not receive what we want, and others behave in ways that we do not like. Approval comes and goes, but love is, by definition, that which is unconditional. Strive today for unconditional love with yourself and with others.

Journaling
Reflections on the Daily Inspiration

___
___
___
___
___
___

April 1

In your relationships, do you focus on what you love about the person or on what you don't like? Which do you offer the most—appreciation or criticism? Since no one will ever meet your idea of perfection, why waste energy on complaints and criticism? If you spend your energy offering love and appreciation, you will find your heart feeling full of love.

Journaling
Reflections on the Daily Inspiration

_____
_____
_____
_____
_____
_____
_____

April 2

The paradox of our wounded self is that it wants to feel safe so it tries in so many ways to control that which it cannot control, which leads to feeling anxious and unsafe. Surrendering to what is and opening to spiritual guidance creates the peace that will never come from trying to control.

Journaling
Reflections on the Daily Inspiration

___
___
___
___
___
___
___

April 3

Today, allow joy to be your guide. Think thoughts that create inner joy. Take actions that create joy. Spirit has given us the experience of joy to let us know when we are on track with our beliefs, thoughts, and actions. Joy is spirit's way of communicating to us that we are thinking and behaving in true and loving ways.

Journaling
Reflections on the Daily Inspiration

April 4

Every time we blame someone, we make them responsible for our feelings and needs, which puts us in the position of being a victim. Every time we blame someone, we disempower ourselves. Today notice the tendency of your wounded self to blame others for your upsets.

Journaling
Reflections on the Daily Inspiration

___
___
___
___
___
___
___

April 5

Today, take some time to write down what love means to you. How do you define love? How are you being when you are being loving to yourself and others? How are others being when they are being loving to you? What does it mean to you to truly love someone? You might want to consider that when you love, you have your own and others' highest good at heart.

Journaling
Reflections on the Daily Inspiration

_____
_____
_____
_____
_____
_____
_____

April 6

Are you afraid to be seen? Are you afraid for someone to look deeply into your eyes and see your soul? Are you afraid that what they will see is nothingness? Your wounded self believes you are empty, nothing. Yet you are a great gift, a child of God, a child of Love. Your soul is love. When you discover this, you will know who you are, and you will no longer be afraid.

Journaling
Reflections on the Daily Inspiration

April 7

Today, notice what you think that causes stress in your body. Stress is the leading cause of illness. Stress causes the immune system to break down. Stress is often caused by your own beliefs, thoughts, and actions regarding circumstances, not just by the circumstances themselves. Today, notice your thoughts that cause stress. Are you sure these thoughts are based on truth?

Journaling
Reflections on the Daily Inspiration

April 8

Love has no expectations of others—it is a free gift of spirit. Today invite love to fill your being and share it with all you meet.

Journaling
Reflections on the Daily Inspiration

April 9

Today, make inner peace your highest priority. Today, sit on the wounded part of you that wants to think thoughts that agitate. Today, think only thoughts that create inner peace. It is a discipline to allow only thoughts that create peace. Today, practice that discipline.

Journaling
Reflections on the Daily Inspiration

April 10

What nurtures you? Do you feel nurtured by being out in nature? By doing something creative? By sitting quietly and listening to music or reading or watching a movie? By being with caring friends? By being physically active—hiking, playing a sport, or gardening? By meditating, journaling, practicing Inner Bonding? By playing fun games? By playing a musical instrument? Today, be sure to create balance in your life by nurturing yourself.

Journaling
Reflections on the Daily Inspiration

_____
_____
_____
_____
_____
_____

April 11

Who is in charge on the inner level—a severe taskmaster, or a loving adult, connected with your spiritual guidance? Does the inner voice say, "You have to do this—get going," or does the inner voice say, "Come on, this can be fun." When you allow your guidance to be in charge, you will move out of resistance and into loving action. Procrastination ends when a loving adult is in charge.

Journaling
Reflections on the Daily Inspiration

April 12

People with entitlement issues often attract those with caretaking issues. The person with the entitlement issue believes he or she deserves to take from others, while the caretaker believes he or she deserves to be taken from. Neither are taking loving care of themselves.

Journaling
Reflections on the Daily Inspiration

_____
_____
_____
_____
_____
_____
_____

April 13

Anxiety is always a sign that you are not in surrender to spirit. Anxiety is the result of attachment to control. We get anxious when we desire control over that which we have no control, when we are not in the moment, and when we are not in faith that we are being guided in our highest good. Today, notice your anxiety and see how it relates to control.

Journaling
Reflections on the Daily Inspiration

___
___
___
___
___
___

April 14

Ponder the difference between knowledge and wisdom. Knowledge is something we acquire through various forms of education—books, experts, the Internet. Wisdom is a deep inner knowing of how to apply the knowledge in ways that support our highest good and the highest good of all. Knowledge without wisdom is the realm of the wounded self. Wisdom is the realm of the loving adult.

Journaling
Reflections on the Daily Inspiration

April 15

If you go deep inside, you will discover that the hope of all addictive, controlling behavior is to protect you from feeling the loneliness of not being connected with another, and from feeling helpless over others and outcomes, and from the heartache and heartbreak of others' unloving behavior. When you learn to accept and manage these feelings with kindness toward yourself and through your connection with spirit, you will discover your wholeness and freedom.

Journaling
Reflections on the Daily Inspiration

___
___
___
___
___
___
___

April 16

If you believe that your painful wounded feelings such as fear, anger, anxiety, depression, hurt, guilt, shame, aloneness, emptiness, or stress are only coming from external sources—such as people, the past or events—then you are stuck being a victim. This week, begin to notice that these feelings may be coming from your own current thoughts, beliefs, and actions.

Journaling
Reflections on the Daily Inspiration

_____
_____
_____
_____
_____
_____
_____

April 17

Notice who you feel responsible for—yourself and/or others. Are you taking responsibility for others' feelings while ignoring your own? Do you believe you can control how others feel? Do others have to be feeling good for you to feel good? Are you making others responsible for your feelings?

Journaling
Reflections on the Daily Inspiration

___
___
___
___
___
___
___

April 18

Acceptance is a great gift to give to yourself and to others—acceptance of talents and of limitations. We each have been given special gifts to offer the world, and we each have our limitations. To be loving means to embrace, value and honor our gifts, and to lovingly accept our limitations.

Journaling
Reflections on the Daily Inspiration

April 19

One of life's greatest challenges is reaching the place where you know, with your whole being, that spirit is supporting and guiding you toward the highest good of your soul. When you know this, you finally let go of control—you let go and let God. This is challenging because the ego wounded self does not want to let go of control and will take every opportunity to undermine your knowingness. Awareness of this inner battle is essential to healing.

Journaling
Reflections on the Daily Inspiration

April 20

Which is your highest priority—safety or love? Is it more important to you to be safe from rejection, engulfment, failure, hurt, or is it more important to you to be a loving person? Are you loving until fear comes up and then retreat to your anger, withdrawal, resistance, or compliance, or do you stay loving and open to learning in the face of fear? Today, notice, which is unconsciously your higher priority—safety or love, and make a conscious choice.

Journaling
Reflections on the Daily Inspiration

April 21

Let Mother Earth nurture you today. Find land to stand on and allow the power of Mother Earth to enliven and strengthen your being. Allow the loving energy of Mother Earth to fill and sustain you. The earth gives much to us—allow her to give to you.

Journaling
Reflections on the Daily Inspiration

_____
_____
_____
_____
_____
_____
_____

April 22

Giving and receiving, receiving and giving, creates a circle of loving energy that fills and brings joy. Giving and receiving, receiving and giving, is an invitation to the joy of spirit. Giving without receiving will eventually leave you drained. Taking without giving will leave you empty. Today, be aware of giving and receiving, receiving and giving with people, animals, nature, and God.

Journaling
Reflections on the Daily Inspiration

___
___
___
___
___
___

April 23

What do you do when you are feeling badly—feeling anxious, hurt, jealous, angry? Do you blame someone else, making others responsible for your feelings? Do you shut down, numb out, use substances or processes to not feel? Instead, try opening to learning about what you are doing or not doing, or what you are telling yourself that is causing you to feel badly. Your upset feelings are a signal that there is some way in which you are abandoning yourself.

Journaling
Reflections on the Daily Inspiration

___
___
___
___
___
___

April 24

Look inside and notice if you feel empty or full. If you feel empty, it is because you are not loving yourself and sharing your love with others. The love-that-is-God fills you when your intent is to love. When your intent is to control getting love, you will feel empty. Notice your intent.

Journaling
Reflections on the Daily Inspiration

_____
_____
_____
_____
_____
_____

April 25

Embrace your wounded feelings of fear, anxiety, anger, and shame with compassion. The moment you move into compassion, your heart opens, and you are able to learn about what would be loving to yourself. Today, focus on compassion for the wounded part of you.

Journaling
Reflections on the Daily Inspiration

_____
_____
_____
_____
_____
_____
_____

April 26

Become conscious of where your focus is. Is it in your mind, trying to figure things out and control things, or is it in your heart, staying connected with your own feelings and with the love and truth of spirit? What is in charge, your mind or your heart, your fear or your love?

Journaling
Reflections on the Daily Inspiration

___
___
___
___
___
___
___

April 27

Today, focus on not taking others' behavior personally. If others are angry, blaming, withdrawn, upset, unavailable, distant—choose to see that their behavior is coming from their own fears and false beliefs rather than being caused by you. We do not cause, nor can we control others' feelings and actions. Today let go of thinking you cause others' feelings and that they cause yours and see how you feel.

Journaling
Reflections on the Daily Inspiration

April 28

When you love someone, you support their joy and freedom. You support what they want for themselves, not what you think they should want or what you want for them. Today, think about if you are really loving others, and who is really loving you.

Journaling
Reflections on the Daily Inspiration

April 29

Your emotions are a great gift, letting you know when you are on track or off track in your thinking and behavior. Today practice learning what your painful emotions are telling you, rather than avoiding them with your various addictions.

Journaling
Reflections on the Daily Inspiration

_____
_____
_____
_____
_____
_____
_____

April 30

Love does not compromise itself. It stays firm even in the face of disapproval, rejection, loss, threats. Love does not fly away in the face of fear. There are no conditions under which love leaves. Notice today how you react in the face of fear.

Journaling
Reflections on the Daily Inspiration

___
___
___
___
___
___
___

May 1

Notice your energy when you greet someone. Do you extend your welcoming out, or do you wait for others to welcome you first? Is your intent to give or to get? Are you hoping others will make you feel safe, or are you creating your own sense of safety?

Journaling
Reflections on the Daily Inspiration

_____
_____
_____
_____
_____
_____
_____

May 2

Today attend to your body, the wonderful house of your soul. Nourish your body with what it really needs—clean pure additive-free and pesticide-free food, clean pure water. Nourish your body with clean pure thoughts, thoughts based on truth rather than on the lies of the wounded self. Nourishing your body creates the frequency for connecting to spirit.

Journaling
Reflections on the Daily Inspiration

___
___
___
___
___
___
___

May 3

If someone's rejecting or controlling behavior triggers your own rejecting or controlling behavior, instead of trying to change the other person, use the situation as an opportunity to heal the fears and false beliefs of your wounded self. Then thank the other person for giving you the opportunity to grow.

Journaling
Reflections on the Daily Inspiration

___
___
___
___
___
___

May 4

Think of a short prayer that you would like to say throughout the day. It can be a prayer of gratitude, a prayer asking for willingness, or for grace, a prayer to be an instrument of love, peace, and joy. Then focus on saying this prayer as often as you can and notice the difference it makes!

Journaling
Reflections on the Daily Inspiration

_____
_____
_____
_____
_____
_____
_____

May 5

What do you do to avoid rejection? Try and be perfect and do everything right? Keep quiet so as not to look stupid? Talk too much to control attention? Today, instead of worrying about being rejected by others, notice how you may be rejecting yourself.

Journaling
Reflections on the Daily Inspiration

___
___
___
___
___
___
___

May 6

Is it more important for you to listen to others or to be heard by others? If it is more important for you to be heard, then you are not hearing yourself—your own inner child. If you are not hearing yourself, then you cannot take loving action for yourself. Today, hear yourself instead of trying to get heard by others.

Journaling
Reflections on the Daily Inspiration

_____
_____
_____
_____
_____
_____
_____

May 7

We often confuse love with indulgence. You are not loving yourself when you indulge in junk food, TV, spending, anger, judgment and so on. You are not loving others when you support them in indulging themselves. Freedom means responsibility. Loving means supporting personal responsibility in yourself and others.

Journaling
Reflections on the Daily Inspiration

___
___
___
___
___
___

May 8

Today, be willing to choose love as your highest priority—higher than avoiding pain, higher than getting love, higher than having control over others and outcomes. When love is your highest priority, you will connect with spirit.

Journaling
Reflections on the Daily Inspiration

___
___
___
___
___
___
___

May 9

Do not be dismayed when you find yourself facing the same issues over and over. We all experience this—it is just different levels of the same soul's lessons. Each time, embrace the issues with compassion.

Journaling
Reflections on the Daily Inspiration

_____
_____
_____
_____
_____
_____
_____

May 10

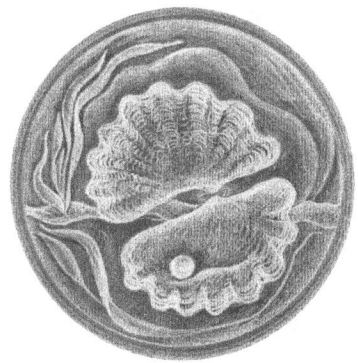

This week, notice if your intent is to get love or approval from others or to give love to yourself and others. Trying to get love or approval will always end up causing suffering. Giving love to yourself and others brings joy.

Journaling
Reflections on the Daily Inspiration

___
___
___
___
___
___
___

May 11

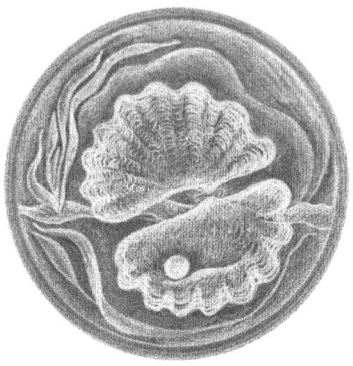

Self-judgment is the way the wounded self tries to control us into doing what we "should" do, what is "right." The wounded self tells us that if we do what we should do, then we can control how others feels about us. However, believing we can control others' feelings is an illusion. All that happens when we judge ourselves is we feel badly. Notice this, without judgment.

Journaling
Reflections on the Daily Inspiration

May 12

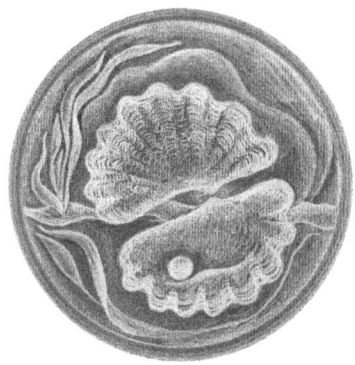

Think about someone you love. Think about who they are without their fear. Can you see their light and love? Can you see their power? Now look within yourself. Who are you without your fear? Today, allow truth to be your guide.

Journaling
Reflections on the Daily Inspiration

May 13

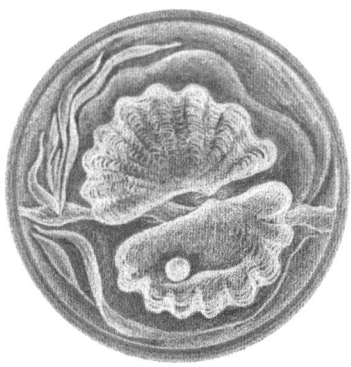

At any moment that you are not connecting with spirit, you might be needy. If you are not being filled with the love that is spirit, you might feel empty. An empty space is a needy space, a space that pulls love and energy from others. Today, put your focus in your heart, choose the intent to learn about love, and open to being filled by the love and grace of spirit.

Journaling
Reflections on the Daily Inspiration

_____
_____
_____
_____
_____
_____
_____

May 14

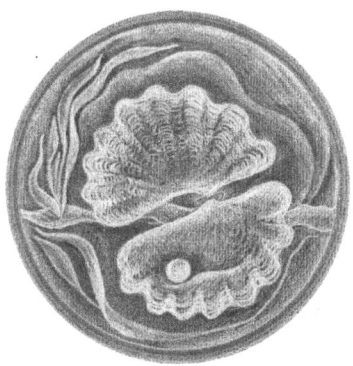

Which is more important to you, safety or intimacy? Safety and intimacy are often mutually exclusive. True intimacy has its up and downs, its closeness and its distance, its peace and its fear, its joy and its sadness. Since there is always the possibility of loss, there is no true safety in intimacy, yet it is the spice of life. Which is more important to you, safety or intimacy?

Journaling
Reflections on the Daily Inspiration

_____
_____
_____
_____
_____
_____
_____

May 15

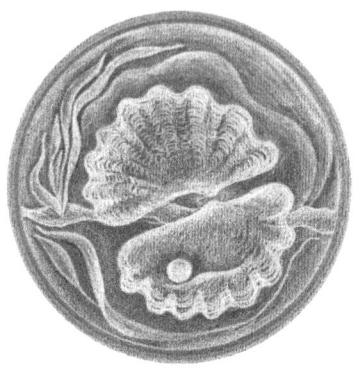

When being loving, we are not grasping, demanding, needy, or clingy because love has nothing to do with getting or taking. We give freely to ourselves and to others. We also receive when the gift is freely given. When being unloving, we may try to manipulate a gift—whether it be of time, money, attention, emotional support, approval, sex, or affection—but when we are loving we know that a gift not freely given is not really a gift. Notice when you are being loving or unloving.

Journaling
Reflections on the Daily Inspiration

May 16

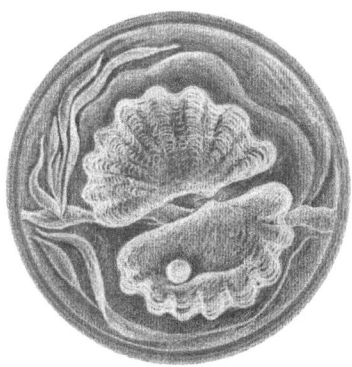

We are all given free will. What does this mean? It does not mean that we can control others and the outcome of things. It means that we have the free will to choose our intention each and every moment. It means that if we choose the intention to protect against fear, we freely choose to behave in unloving ways to ourselves and others. It means if we choose the intention to learn about love, even in the face of fear, we freely choose to be loving to ourselves and others. Free will gives us the ability to choose our intention.

Journaling
Reflections on the Daily Inspiration

_____
_____
_____
_____
_____
_____

May 17

Every kind act to yourself adds kindness to the world. Every kind act to another adds kindness to the world. We each have the power to change the world through our individual acts of kindness to ourselves and others. We are not powerless to bring kindness to ourselves and others. We are not powerless to bring about a more loving world, but the changes must start within you.

Journaling
Reflections on the Daily Inspiration

May 18

Do you love your work? If you don't love your work, you might want to open to learning about what other work might bring you joy. Your soul self, your essence—your inner child—has the blueprint for what you came to the planet to offer. Opening to feeling and hearing your inner child can lead to work that fulfills your heart and soul.

Journaling
Reflections on the Daily Inspiration

_____
_____
_____
_____
_____
_____

May 19

What are you avoiding embracing about yourself so as not to feel different? Are there special gifts and ways of being that you fear will set you apart and cause you to feel left out and lonely? Today, have the courage to look deeply inside and begin to embrace the gifts you have been given.

Journaling
Reflections on the Daily Inspiration

May 20

Seek to be with like-minded people. Your own growth is supported by being with others who are striving to become whole and loving. Love yourself enough to not force yourself to be around close-hearted people, even if they are family or friends.

Journaling
Reflections on the Daily Inspiration

___
___
___
___
___
___
___

May 21

Inner peace is a precious thing—a gift of spirit. You will have inner peace instead of inner turmoil when you allow spirit to guide you instead of needing to control from your own limited mind. You will have inner peace when you allow the truth of spirit to guide you instead of the false beliefs of your wounded self. You will have inner peace when you have the courage to take loving action for yourself—action guided by spirit.

Journaling
Reflections on the Daily Inspiration

_____
_____
_____
_____
_____
_____

May 22

Is there some loving action you have been putting off? Today, stop procrastinating and take the loving action. It is only through taking action on your own behalf that your inner child will feel important to you and valued and loved by you. Your inner child believes the actions, not the words.

Journaling
Reflections on the Daily Inspiration

___
___
___
___
___
___
___

May 23

Today, ponder the sacredness of this incredible opportunity to be on this planet and evolve your soul in love. Allow yourself to feel awe at the wonder of being in a body, able to experience the beauty of nature and the opportunity to share love in many different ways. Untold numbers of souls are waiting to come here. Embrace gratitude for the sacred privilege of being here.

Journaling
Reflections on the Daily Inspiration

___
___
___
___
___
___

May 24

Today, put your attention on being kind—kind to your self, to others, to the planet. Kindness is a doorway to spirit. You will find if you put your whole focus on being kind, your heart will stay open, and you will feel the love of spirit with you.

Journaling
Reflections on the Daily Inspiration

_____
_____
_____
_____
_____
_____
_____

May 25

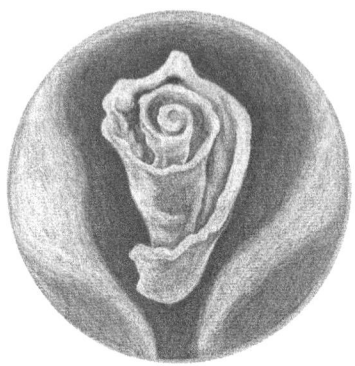

Today, every time you feel any anxiety, say a brief prayer of gratitude—even for something simple like the light from a lamp, or a soft tissue to sneeze into. Then invite spirit into your heart and you will notice your anxiety subsiding. Then, open to learning about what the anxiety is telling you about how you are treating yourself.

Journaling
Reflections on the Daily Inspiration

_____
_____
_____
_____
_____
_____
_____

May 26

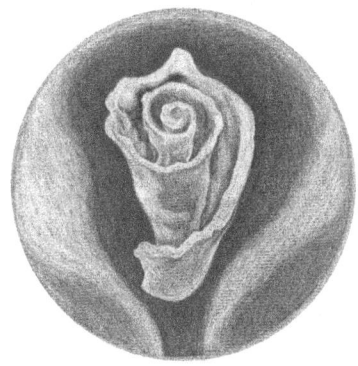

Change is a challenge for many of us. We feel safe when things are predictable, yet change is a fact of life and gives life it's spice. Today, embrace change in your life, especially change within yourself.

Journaling
Reflections on the Daily Inspiration

___
___
___
___
___
___
___

May 27

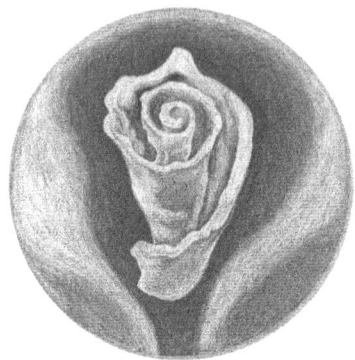

Perfectionism is just another form of control. "If I am perfect, then I can have control over how others feel about me and treat me" Life becomes much easier when we let go of having to be perfect and allow ourselves to be human.

Journaling
Reflections on the Daily Inspiration

May 28

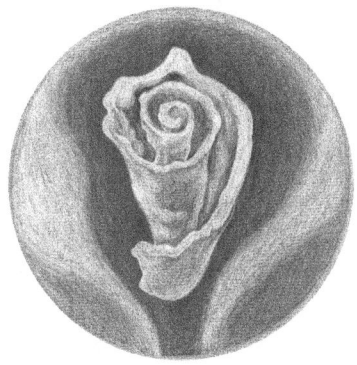

Tune into what you *really* want and dream big! If what you really want doesn't scare you, your dream is not big enough! Then write it down, plan how to get there, and stay focused on the joy of your dream so spirit can help you manifest it!

Journaling
Reflections on the Daily Inspiration

___
___
___
___
___
___
___

May 29

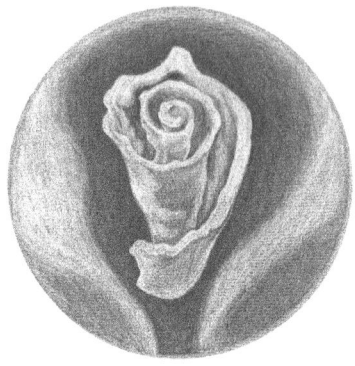

When you are in your body and present in this moment, you are able to pick up information that you cannot perceive from your mind. You become aware of energies that give you direct knowing about others and situations. This creates much more safety than trying to control.

Journaling
Reflections on the Daily Inspiration

___
___
___
___
___
___

May 30

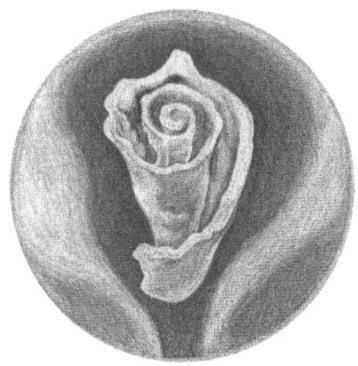

Anything can become an addiction, depending upon your intent. Today notice, without judgment, your addictions—the things you do to avoid your feelings of aloneness, loneliness, heartbreak, and helplessness over others. Notice substances, activities, and behaviors toward others. Ask yourself, "Am I doing this because it is loving to myself and supports the highest good of my soul's journey, or am I doing this to avoid taking responsibility for my feelings?"

Journaling
Reflections on the Daily Inspiration

_____
_____
_____
_____
_____
_____

May 31

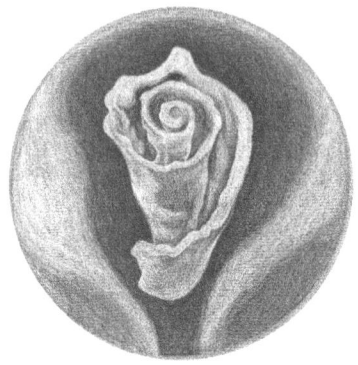

Love, compassion, truth, and peace are not experiences that are generated from our own minds. They are gifts of spirit that come to us when we are truly open to learning about what is most loving to ourselves and others.

Journaling
Reflections on the Daily Inspiration

_____
_____
_____
_____
_____
_____
_____

June 1

When is the last time you scheduled time for play, for creativity, or to do nothing? For many of us, our lives are out of balance. Today, focus on creating balance between work and play, between activity and rest, between doing and being.

Journaling
Reflections on the Daily Inspiration

June 2

Control or love—which intent are you choosing right now? Suffering or joy—which result are you experiencing right now? Today, focus on letting go of the illusion of control over others and outcomes and focus instead on what you CAN control—your own intent!

Journaling
Reflections on the Daily Inspiration

June 3

We all have challenges in our lives. The real challenge is: how do we walk through challenges? The challenge is to not let challenges get you off track. When challenges come your way, accept the challenge of staying in faith, letting go of the outcome, staying connected with your guidance, and praying for the highest good of all.

Journaling
Reflections on the Daily Inspiration

June 4

The love of God is expressed through each of us. Who needs your help today? Who needs your encouragement, your smile, your presence? Who needs you to listen, hear and understand? Whose day can you contribute to today with your loving presence?

Journaling
Reflections on the Daily Inspiration

June 5

Energy is everything. Energy always follows intent. When your intent is to learn, your energy will be light and easy. When your intent is to protect against pain or control others and outcomes or your own feelings, your energy will be heavy and dark. When your intent is to learn about loving yourself—loving your own inner child—and sharing your love with others, you will be able to discern another's intent to control or to learn. This creates inner safety.

Journaling
Reflections on the Daily Inspiration

_____
_____
_____
_____
_____
_____
_____

June 6

Are you attached to being right as a way to control how others feel about you and treat you? Do you hesitate to speak your truth because you want to be sure you are right? Protecting yourself from others' disapproval by being right is not loving to yourself. It is loving to yourself to speak your truth, without judgment, and then courageously deal with the results.

Journaling
Reflections on the Daily Inspiration

June 7

Today, choose kindness as your guide: Kindness toward your inner child—your emotions; Kindness toward your body; Kindness toward others; Kindness toward Mother Earth. Let kindness be your guiding light today, and each day.

Journaling
Reflections on the Daily Inspiration

_____
_____
_____
_____
_____
_____
_____

June 8

Loving action is always true to ourselves. Any action that denies our truth is an unloving action. Giving—of time, money, sex, approval—when we do not want to give is unloving to ourselves and others. Notice if you are giving to get or giving for the joy of it.

Journaling
Reflections on the Daily Inspiration

_____
_____
_____
_____
_____
_____

June 9

Notice your thoughts. Your thoughts are like magnets, attracting to you a like energy. Your negative thoughts, based on false beliefs, attract darkness, creating anxiety and fear. Your positive thoughts, based on truth, attract love and abundance. Notice your thoughts.

Journaling
Reflections on the Daily Inspiration

___
___
___
___
___
___
___

June 10

When we operate from fear and a desire to control, we might be bringing about the very things we want to avoid. Today, notice how attempting to control others—to get approval, time, sex, and so on—may create resistance in others.

Journaling
Reflections on the Daily Inspiration

June 11

We do not cause others to feel and behave the way they do, nor do others cause us to feel and behave the way we do. Each of us has the free will to choose in each moment to be honest or dishonest, open or closed, accepting or judgmental, loving or unloving. Today, let go of trying to control others' feelings and behavior, and let go of blaming others for yours.

Journaling
Reflections on the Daily Inspiration

June 12

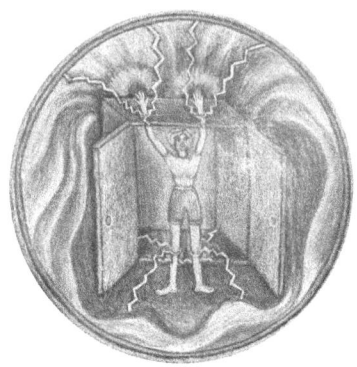

Today, focus on letting go of all desire for attention, approval, appreciation, or love from others. Focus on giving yourself attention, approval, appreciation, and love.

Journaling
Reflections on the Daily Inspiration

_____
_____
_____
_____
_____
_____
_____

June 13

Who defines your worth? Is your worth defined by others' approval, attention, and validation? Today, open to spirit for the definition of your true worth. Ask your guidance who you really are and treat yourself as the child of God that you are.

Journaling
Reflections on the Daily Inspiration

June 14

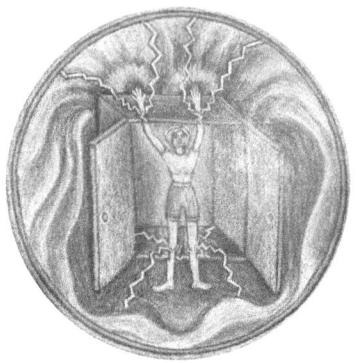

Notice whether judging yourself motivates you. Do you feel more energized or less when you judge yourself? Are you clearer and more creative when you judge yourself, or does the tension created by self-judgment block your clarity and creativity? Does self-judgment create peace or stress? Notice whether you are operating under the illusion that stress works well for you.

Journaling
Reflections on the Daily Inspiration

June 15

Listen. Listen to the trees. Listen to the rocks. Listen to the animals. Listen in the quietness of yourself. Spirit is speaking to you each moment. Listen, and you will find your joy.

Journaling
Reflections on the Daily Inspiration

June 16

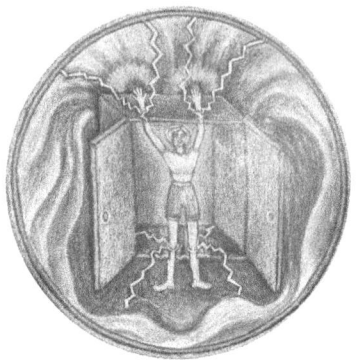

Look for beauty everywhere—in people, in animals, in nature, in works of art and in everyday objects, environments and experiences. Allow yourself to be fully present with everything you encounter, and to feel your love and gratitude for the beauty. This opens you to oneness with God.

Journaling
Reflections on the Daily Inspiration

_____
_____
_____
_____
_____
_____
_____

June 17

When someone has hurt you deeply and you just want to get back at him or her, ask yourself: What is the high road? What is truly loving to yourself? Will hurting another really help you?

Journaling
Reflections on the Daily Inspiration

___
___
___
___
___
___
___

June 18

We all want connection. We don't want to feel alone and lonely and we have many addictions to avoid these feelings. Yet the moment we connect with spirit and with ourselves, we do not feel alone, and then we can manage the loneliness of not being connected with others. Today, do not leave your inner child alone. Bring the love of spirit to your child so that you can manage the moments of loneliness as they arise.

Journaling
Reflections on the Daily Inspiration

June 19

A key to success is to live in complete integrity. This means: To speak your truth. To create balance between work and play. To stay connected with spiritual guidance. To stay open to learning within yourself and with others. To take full responsibility for your own feelings, health, and well-being—to not be victim of others' choices. Strive to live each day in complete integrity.

Journaling
Reflections on the Daily Inspiration

_____
_____
_____
_____
_____
_____

June 20

How often are you present in this moment? It is only when you are present that you feel the presence of spirit within—which is your true soul self. Today, practice being in this moment—with yourself, with nature, and with others.

Journaling
Reflections on the Daily Inspiration

_____
_____
_____
_____
_____
_____
_____

June 21

Who triggers your anger? Who triggers your withdrawal? Who triggers your feeling like a victim? Who triggers your resistance? These people are your teachers. They activate your wounds, your unhealed false beliefs. Notice these wounds, embrace them, learn about them, and bring in the truth from spirit to heal them. Then thank the people in your life who trigger your wounds—they are your teachers.

Journaling
Reflections on the Daily Inspiration

_____
_____
_____
_____
_____
_____
_____

June 22

A gift is not a gift unless there are no strings attached, no need to get anything back. If you expect gratitude, approval, a thank you, or if you expect the person to like it, wear it, use it—it is not a gift, it is a manipulation. Notice your intent when you give a gift—to give or to get.

Journaling
Reflections on the Daily Inspiration

June 23

How often do you refrain from speaking up for yourself because you don't want to hurt someone, or you are afraid someone will get angry? Not speaking up for yourself is a way to control others' feelings and behavior. Today, notice without judgment all the times you do not speak up for yourself, and how you feel as a result.

Journaling
Reflections on the Daily Inspiration

June 24

How often do you tell yourself that what you want and feel and need is not important? How often do you make others' wants and feelings and needs more important than your own? How often do you notice that you are feeling angry and resentful as a result? This is your inner child angry at you for not loving him or her. Today, notice this without judgment, with a compassionate intent to learn.

Journaling
Reflections on the Daily Inspiration

June 25

Love, peace and joy are gifts of spirit. We do not create them ourselves. They enter our hearts when we open our hearts to spirit by focusing on what is loving to ourselves and others.

Journaling
Reflections on the Daily Inspiration

June 26

We are created in the image of God which is Love. Our essence is love, the same love that is God. We are not our fears, our false beliefs, or our many protections. Today, remember who you are. Remember the spark of the Divine, which is who you are and manifest this upon the planet.

Journaling
Reflections on the Daily Inspiration

June 27

Today, notice everything you do that you value. Tell your inner child out loud things like, "Thank you, that was a very caring thing to do." "I appreciate your sense of humor." "I love your ideas. Thank you for your creativity." "You are a really loving person." Your inner child needs to be seen for who he or she really is, not just for looks or performance.

Journaling
Reflections on the Daily Inspiration

___
___
___
___
___
___

June 28

Are you listening to the quiet voice of your spiritual guidance? Are you attending to the flashes of ideas, words, pictures, and feelings that are always coming through to you from your guidance? Today, focus on being present with the quietness of your guidance.

Journaling
Reflections on the Daily Inspiration

_____
_____
_____
_____
_____
_____
_____

June 29

Our wounded self—our ego—cannot discern the truth. It operates only from learned limiting beliefs. Truth comes from spirit. Today, challenge yourself to operate from truth instead of from fear.

Journaling
Reflections on the Daily Inspiration

_____
_____
_____
_____
_____
_____
_____

June 30

We want to believe that we can control how others feel about us. We want to believe that if we just do it right, look right, say the right thing, perform right, we can control how others feel about us. Today, accept this as an illusion and just be who you are.

Journaling
Reflections on the Daily Inspiration

July 1

Do you believe that another person can fill your emptiness and make you feel loved and safe? Has this worked for you? Today, focus on filling yourself up with spirit and doing all you can to make your own inner child feel loved and safe, and see how you end up feeling.

Journaling
Reflections on the Daily Inspiration

July 2

Send blessings of love to those around you who are grumpy, angry, blaming or withdrawn. Reassure your inner child that others' behavior is not personal to you. Remember that you can help others with your love, but you cannot change their intent.

Journaling
Reflections on the Daily Inspiration

_____
_____
_____
_____
_____
_____
_____

July 3

Notice your level of honesty or dishonesty. Do you elaborate or bend the truth about yourself to control how others feel about you? Are you brutally honest about how you feel toward others as a means of controlling them? Notice that honesty can be used both lovingly and as a means of control, depending upon your intent.

Journaling
Reflections on the Daily Inspiration

July 4

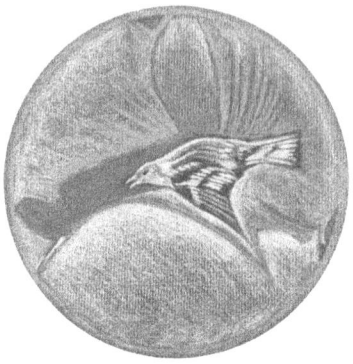

If you are in the habit of telling others your feelings and wanting others to hear your feelings, notice your intent in telling your feelings. Are you wanting others to take responsibility for your feelings, or are you sharing your feelings to get help in taking responsibility for your own feelings?

Journaling
Reflections on the Daily Inspiration

_____
_____
_____
_____
_____
_____
_____

July 5

Do you sometimes feel empty? The only thing that fills emptiness is love, and love comes through us from spirit. The next time you feel empty, open to learning about what is loving and caring to you and others and you will start to feel the fullness of love that comes from spirit.

Journaling
Reflections on the Daily Inspiration

___
___
___
___
___
___
___

July 6

Our feelings of peace and joy let us know we are on the right track—that we are taking loving care of ourselves. Notice what thoughts and actions create peace. Notice what thoughts and actions bring joy. Let your peace and joy be your beacons to the light.

Journaling
Reflections on the Daily Inspiration

_____
_____
_____
_____
_____
_____
_____

July 7

Do you often go along with what someone else wants you to do instead of checking in with your feelings and your guidance to see what you want and what is in your highest good? You might want to notice that giving yourself up often creates depression and apathy. Today, take the risk of being loving to yourself rather than giving yourself up to others and notice how you feel.

Journaling
Reflections on the Daily Inspiration

_____
_____
_____
_____
_____
_____
_____

July 8

The energy of your soul is huge and not confined to the limits of your body. If too much of your soul energy is trapped with other people and in other places, you will feel tired, joyless, and scattered. Today, open your heart to bringing home your scattered soul parts from family, friends, and places. Spirit will assist you when your intent is to be whole.

Journaling
Reflections on the Daily Inspiration

_____
_____
_____
_____
_____
_____
_____

July 9

When our intent is to learn, we are able to hear the truth from others, even when it is difficult. This does not mean that we do not express pain or fear when the truth is hurtful or scary, but that if these feelings arise, we handle them responsibly. When we become a safe receptacle for truth, others will naturally tell us the truth. Notice if you are willing to hear the truth.

Journaling
Reflections on the Daily Inspiration

_____
_____
_____
_____
_____
_____

July 10

The higher your frequency, the easier time you will have in hearing your spiritual guidance. Fear, hurt, anger, anxiety, judgment, depression, as well as sugar, drugs, alcohol, lots of food, heavy food, and controlling behavior lower your frequency. Love, laughter, joy, peace, pure foods, and the intent to learn raise your frequency. Today notice this.

Journaling
Reflections on the Daily Inspiration

_____
_____
_____
_____
_____
_____

July 11

Are you willing to tell the total truth about yourself, even in the face of fear or loss of love from another? Love does not attempt to manipulate a loved one with niceness, diplomacy, white lies, explanations, or complaints to avoid their anger, disapproval, or loss of the relationship. These tactics arise from fear, and since love and fear do not coexist, it is impossible to lie about ourselves when we approach the world with an open heart.

Journaling
Reflections on the Daily Inspiration

_____
_____
_____
_____
_____
_____
_____

July 12

Relationship problems center around control. The wounded self always wants to be in control and not be controlled. Today, notice with compassion the part of you that wants to control and the part of you that resists being controlled. Then, instead of controlling or resisting, open to guidance about what is in your highest good.

Journaling
Reflections on the Daily Inspiration

_____
_____
_____
_____
_____
_____

July 13

Today, notice where your focus is most of the time—externally on others, in your head, or in your body. Since your feelings are your inner guidance system, it is essential to be present in your body in order to know what you are feeling and when you need to take loving action.

Journaling
Reflections on the Daily Inspiration

_____
_____
_____
_____
_____
_____
_____

July 14

We all need reminders throughout the day to remember love, remember spirit, remember God. Today, sprinkle your home, your car, and your workspace with little reminders—notes, flowers, and small objects of beauty to remind you to open your heart to learning and loving.

Journaling
Reflections on the Daily Inspiration

July 15

Embrace with compassion your wounded feelings of anxiety, fear, depression, anger, jealousy, guilt, shame, aloneness, rage, blame. Hold your inner child and explore what you are thinking or doing that is causing these feelings. What are you telling yourself? All thoughts that create suffering are lies to ourselves, coming from our false beliefs. Discover the thoughts that are creating your suffering. Pain is a part of life, but emotional suffering is a choice that results from our untrue thoughts.

Journaling
Reflections on the Daily Inspiration

_____
_____
_____
_____
_____
_____

July 16

When you feel great, enjoy it! When you feel bad, explore it. Your painful feelings are letting you know that you are off track, that you are thinking things that are not true. This is how our guidance lets us know we are off track in our thinking. When we are joyful, we are on track, coming from truth. When we are in pain, we are off track, coming from fear. Exploring will lead you to the truth and back into joy.

Journaling
Reflections on the Daily Inspiration

_____
_____
_____
_____
_____
_____

July 17

How often is kindness your highest priority? How often do you get angry or blaming toward a partner or a child for a minor infraction, making being right or having control more important than kindness? Today, focus on being kind to yourself and others and notice how much happier you are!

Journaling
Reflections on the Daily Inspiration

___
___
___
___
___

July 18

Our greatest freedom resides on our ability to choose our intent. You will not feel free when you choose the intent to control, and choose to be unconscious of this choice. You will feel an incredible freedom when you consciously choose, moment by moment, the intent to learn about love.

Journaling
Reflections on the Daily Inspiration

July 19

Today, notice the funny side of things. Let go of taking things so seriously and laugh at the absurdities of life. Lighten up with laughter. Laughter heals and enlightens body and soul. Today, open to the gift of laughter and create the lightness of being that opens you to spirit.

Journaling
Reflections on the Daily Inspiration

_____
_____
_____
_____
_____
_____

July 20

Today, be very conscious of your energy. Your energy gives to the planet, or takes from it, adds to the peace, or adds to the fear. Your peace and joy add to the peace and joy of the planet, while your anger, fear, blame, and judgment exacerbate these negative energies on the planet. Each of us is responsible for our energy each moment.

Journaling
Reflections on the Daily Inspiration

_____
_____
_____
_____
_____
_____

July 21

Today, notice what you do to avoid painful feelings. Do you stay in your head instead of in your body? Do you keep your breath shallow? Do you get angry, withdrawn, judgmental? Do you use food, alcohol, drugs, sex, spending, gambling, work, TV, the Internet? Today, embrace and learn from your feelings instead of avoiding them and find your peace.

Journaling
Reflections on the Daily Inspiration

_____
_____
_____
_____
_____
_____

July 22

Today, seek spirit through connection with others. It is easy to know God when sharing love with others. Open your heart to the sharing of love and seek out those with open hearts. You will most deeply experience God not in the getting of love, or the offering of love, but in the sharing of love.

Journaling
Reflections on the Daily Inspiration

_____
_____
_____
_____
_____
_____
_____

July 23

Ask yourself with each choice you make today, "Would I want this announced on the Internet?" Staying in integrity means thinking and behaving in ways you are proud of. Be vigilant about your integrity and it will move you into the light.

Journaling
Reflections on the Daily Inspiration

_____
_____
_____
_____
_____
_____
_____

July 24

Your intent to control or to love governs everything. Loving means you are surrendered to being guided by spirit. Controlling means you are caught in your own mind, with fear, anger, obsessive thoughts, false beliefs. Which are you choosing in this moment?

Journaling
Reflections on the Daily Inspiration

___
___
___
___
___
___
___

July 25

Consciously notice and think about what you are grateful for and what brings you joy. Notice how you feel when your thoughts are on what you want rather than on what you don't want.

Journaling
Reflections on the Daily Inspiration

___
___
___
___
___
___
___

July 26

If you do not cherish your body, your inner child will not feel loved. Your child lives in your body and expresses through your body. If you don't feed your body well, if you don't get enough sleep or enough exercise or enough downtime to regenerate, your child will not feel loved and cherished. Today, cherish your body, the temple of your soul.

Journaling
Reflections on the Daily Inspiration

_____
_____
_____
_____
_____
_____
_____

July 27

If someone close to you is often pulling on you for love, approval, attention, you might want to notice if you are in resistance. If someone close to you is often in resistance, you might want to look at how you might be pulling with some form of control. The pull-resist system in relationships is circular.

Journaling
Reflections on the Daily Inspiration

_____
_____
_____
_____
_____
_____

July 28

Being open to learning sometimes means learning about our wounded self, the part of us that wants to control everything. Being open to learning sometimes means embracing the journey of discovering our many layers of controlling behaviors. If you judge yourself for controlling, then the journey gets stuck. If you make it okay to be controlling, then the journey becomes an exciting adventure of discovery and healing.

Journaling
Reflections on the Daily Inspiration

_____
_____
_____
_____
_____
_____
_____

July 29

Earth is a challenging place to be and will be filled with pain for you unless you stay in conscious connection with the love, wisdom, guidance, and comfort of the Divine Mother/Father spirit that is within you and around you and always available to you. Today, focus on connecting with this love.

Journaling
Reflections on the Daily Inspiration

___
___
___
___
___
___

July 30

The decision to want responsibility for your feelings and your wellbeing is what makes your inner child feel loved, valued, and worthy! Without this wanting, your inner child feels abandoned, even when being loved by another or others.

Journaling
Reflections on the Daily Inspiration

_____
_____
_____
_____
_____
_____
_____

July 31

Today, notice *without judgment*, if you are primarily a taker—expecting others to take care of you, or if you are primarily a caretaker—taking care of others in the hopes they will love you and connect to you. Both are aspects of the wounded self and are symptoms of self-abandonment.

Journaling
Reflections on the Daily Inspiration

August 1

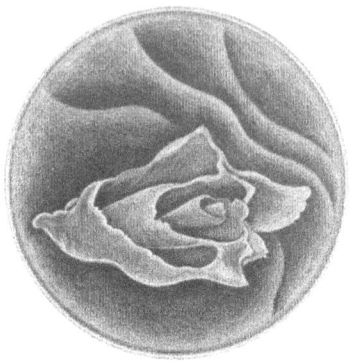

Today, embrace all adversity as an opportunity to learn. All adversity has within it the seed of learning and growth. If you approach adversity as a victim, you will not learn the lesson it is here to teach you. If you embrace it with an intent to learn, you will be astounded at the gifts it has for you.

Journaling
Reflections on the Daily Inspiration

_____
_____
_____
_____
_____
_____

August 2

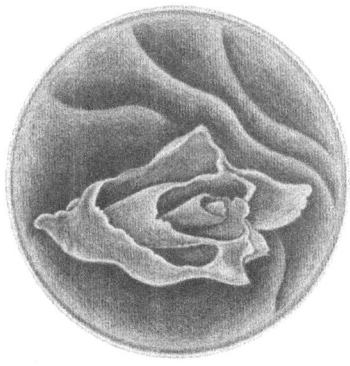

Judgments, whether toward yourself or others, often create resistance. Others pick up your judgmental energy even if you don't say anything. Today, notice your judgmental thoughts and replace them with kind, compassionate thoughts.

Journaling
Reflections on the Daily Inspiration

_____
_____
_____
_____
_____
_____
_____

August 3

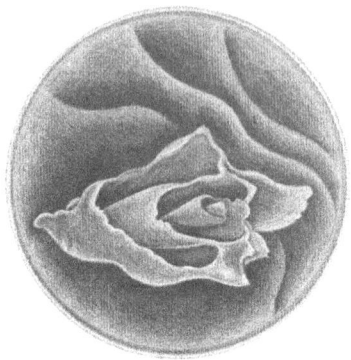

As you go through your day, who are you being? Are you being the kindness, joy, compassion, and peace of your beautiful essence? Or are you being the anger, fear, judgment, anxiety, and depression of your wounded self? Free will means you get to choose who you want to be, each and every moment. Today be conscious of that choice.

Journaling
Reflections on the Daily Inspiration

_____
_____
_____
_____
_____
_____
_____

August 4

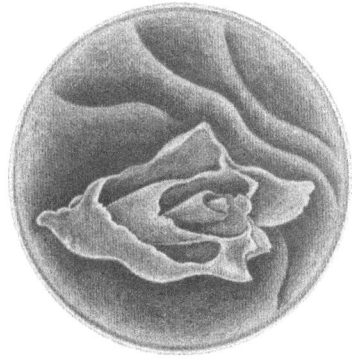

The loving adult tells the truth. Focus on the untruths you may be telling yourself about having control over others and the outcome of things. Ask your guidance for the truth.

Journaling
Reflections on the Daily Inspiration

_____
_____
_____
_____
_____
_____
_____

August 5

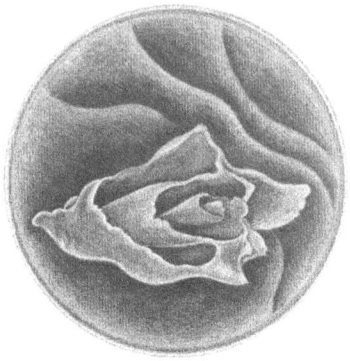

How would life be different for you if you lived in faith—faith that spirit is always supporting your highest good, faith that your soul is immortal, faith that life on this planet is about a spiritual journey of evolving toward love? What worries would you let go of if you lived in faith that you are never alone, that you are always being supported by your higher guidance?

Journaling
Reflections on the Daily Inspiration

_____
_____
_____
_____
_____
_____

August 6

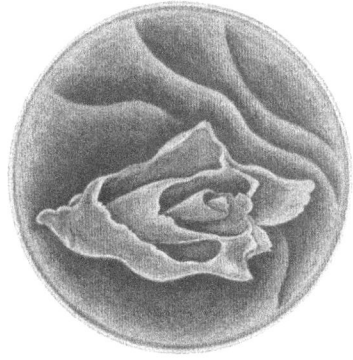

The desire to not be controlled is so great in many people that it often overrides caring. When you feel pulled at by someone to do what they want, do you go into automatic resistance? Next time you feel the pull, stop and ask yourself, "What is in my highest good, to do what this person wants or not?" That way you are making your own choices rather than being controlled by your resistance.

Journaling
Reflections on the Daily Inspiration

___
___
___
___
___
___

August 7

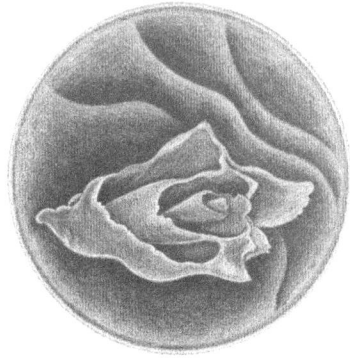

Today, slow down. Breathe. Walk more slowly. Be present to yourself, to others, to your environment, and to spirit. Each moment you are truly present is a moment of enlightenment.

Journaling
Reflections on the Daily Inspiration

_____
_____
_____
_____
_____
_____
_____
_____

August 8

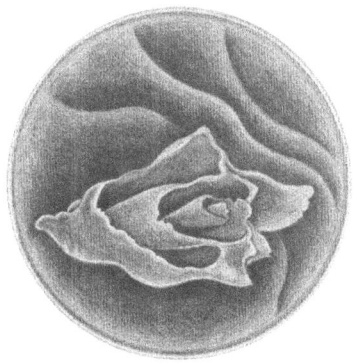

Notice what opens your heart and soul. Nature, you garden, your child, your pet? Your grandchild, your creativity, music, art? Walking, running, sharing, loving? Sexuality, sensuality, affection, holding? What melts the wall, enlivens your being, tickles your tummy, and fills your heart? Notice and make time for that which opens your heart.

Journaling
Reflections on the Daily Inspiration

___
___
___
___
___
___

August 9

Relationships bring up every unhealed issue we have. Just because you may be having a hard time in your relationship does not mean it is time to leave it. You take your patterns with you wherever you go. The important thing is—are you both open to learning about and healing these patterns?

Journaling
Reflections on the Daily Inspiration

_____
_____
_____
_____
_____
_____
_____

August 10

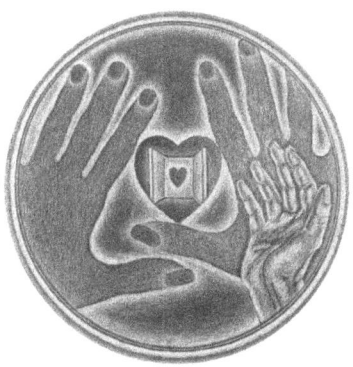

Notice your judgments towards others. Each time you notice one, notice how it makes you feel when you judge. Are you judging yourself in a similar way? Notice how that makes you feel. Ask your guidance if any of your judgments are truth, or are they coming from false beliefs, and ask what is true?

Journaling
Reflections on the Daily Inspiration

___
___
___
___
___
___

August 11

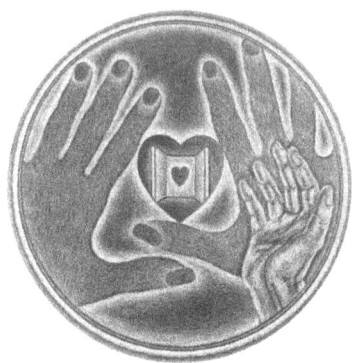

"Peace begins with me." This week, take this to heart by focusing on creating inner peace through thinking peaceful thoughts and taking peaceful actions toward yourself and others. The moment you have anxiety, notice the thoughts creating it and bring your thoughts back to the truth, which creates inner peace.

Journaling
Reflections on the Daily Inspiration

August 12

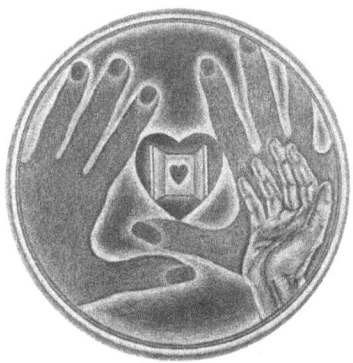

How much of your thinking time is about love? Today, seek to learn about love from your inner guidance, your higher guidance, and from wise others. Today, seek to love in each and every thought and action, and to remember to learn about love with every challenge to your peace.

Journaling
Reflections on the Daily Inspiration

August 13

Controlling behavior is neither good nor bad—it just does not serve us well. It was part of our survival as children and now is causing much of our pain. Noticing your controlling behavior with compassion and curiosity rather than with judgment, puts you on the fast lane to healing.

Journaling
Reflections on the Daily Inspiration

_____
_____
_____
_____
_____
_____
_____

August 14

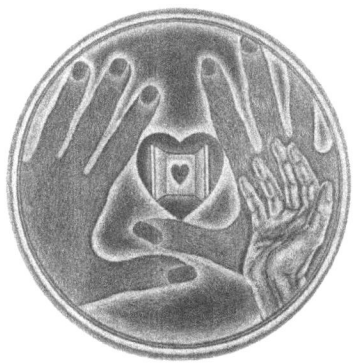

His little inner child came to him in pain and emptiness. He filled the emptiness with alcohol. His little inner child felt abandoned, so he turned on the TV. As long as his intent was to avoid taking responsibility for his own pain and emptiness, he continued to create the very pain and emptiness he was trying to avoid.

Journaling
Reflections on the Daily Inspiration

_____
_____
_____
_____
_____
_____

August 15

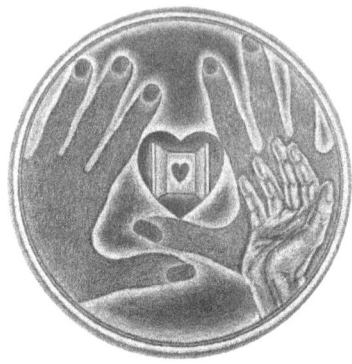

Being safe is not about controlling others and outcomes. Being safe is not about staying in the mind and figuring things out. You will feel safe when you connect with your spiritual guidance, who has your well-being at heart at all times, and will guide you toward those actions and situations that support your safety and highest good.

Journaling
Reflections on the Daily Inspiration

___
___
___
___
___
___

August 16

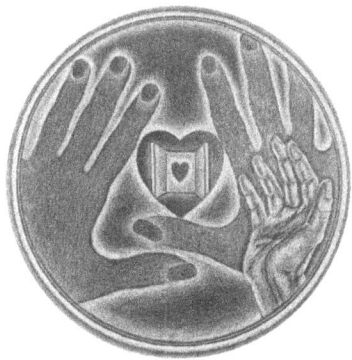

Become willing to learn with and choose to be with those who are also willing to learn. When two or more are gathered with a willingness to learn about love, there is the deep joyousness of connection.

Journaling
Reflections on the Daily Inspiration

___
___
___
___
___
___

August 17

Our spiritual guidance is here to help us, not to control us. Spirit is loving, not invasive. Spirit will guide you towards your peace and joy, and the full manifestation of your gifts when your deepest intent is to be a loving human being, starting with loving yourself.

Journaling
Reflections on the Daily Inspiration

___
___
___
___
___
___

August 18

Today, notice what is more important to you—trying to get others to like you or loving yourself. If you are devoted to having control over how others' feel about you, notice how much energy this takes!

Journaling
Reflections on the Daily Inspiration

_____
_____
_____
_____
_____
_____
_____

August 19

Today, notice with deep gratitude the things you may have that many others do not have: your eyes to see, your ears to hear, your hands and fingers with which to pick up things and to write or type, your legs and feet to walk upon. Be grateful for being able to tie your shoes and for having shoes to tie. Choosing gratitude each moment fills your heart and soul with love.

Journaling
Reflections on the Daily Inspiration

_____
_____
_____
_____
_____
_____

August 20

Today, be honest with yourself—what is more important to you than being a loving human being with yourself and others? Is it to get love, safety, attention, pleasure, power, control, security, approval? Is it to avoid pain, failure, disapproval, engulfment, conflict? Today, notice your intent—to get love and avoid pain, or to be open to learning about loving yourself and others.

Journaling
Reflections on the Daily Inspiration

August 21

None of us heals alone. The wounded self believes we have to go it alone, but part of the job of the loving adult is to reach out for help when help is needed. Today, reach out and receive the help you may be needing.

Journaling
Reflections on the Daily Inspiration

August 22

Notice and appreciate your positive thoughts and behavior. Notice your smile, your kindness, generosity, creativity, humor, caring, understanding, compassion, inner knowing, empathy, integrity, honesty, courage, and the sharing of your love. Notice and appreciate your inner qualities, who you really are, your true soul essence.

Journaling
Reflections on the Daily Inspiration

August 23

Today, focus on your physical health. Are you conscious of what you eat? Are you getting enough exercise and sleep? Are you noticing the thoughts that cause stress? Today, practice becoming conscious of your physical well-being.

Journaling
Reflections on the Daily Inspiration

_____
_____
_____
_____
_____
_____
_____

August 24

Within our souls is the blueprint for our passion and purpose. Opening to learning with your essence, your true self, can guide you to the joy of manifesting your passion and purpose.

Journaling
Reflections on the Daily Inspiration

___
___
___
___
___
___
___

August 25

What is more important to you, safety or aliveness? What is more important to you, safety or intimacy? What is more important to you, safety or integrity? What is more important to you, safety or courage? Today, step out of your safety zone and open to your aliveness, integrity, courage, and to intimacy.

Journaling
Reflections on the Daily Inspiration

_____
_____
_____
_____
_____
_____
_____

August 26

Today, pretend that a video camera in on you, photographing every action, every word, as a role model of loving action for the children of the world to see. With this in mind, you might be more mindful of your intent, of who you choose to be each and every moment.

Journaling
Reflections on the Daily Inspiration

___
___
___
___
___
___
___

August 27

If you are in a relationship, you might think that you are much further along than your partner, or that your partner is much farther along than you. But we are attracted to each other at our common level of woundedness—which is our common level of self-abandonment, as well as our common level of emotional health—which is our common level of self-acceptance and self-love. Today, let go of one-up, one-down thinking.

Journaling
Reflections on the Daily Inspiration

August 28

Are you always busy? Do you have a busyness addiction? Is being busy a way you avoid feelings of loneliness and aloneness? Today, stop the busyness and feel what is happening within. Lovingly embrace whatever painful feelings you discover, then explore them or release them to spirit.

Journaling
Reflections on the Daily Inspiration

_____
_____
_____
_____
_____
_____

August 29

What brings you joy? What makes you laugh? What delights you? What brings you peace? What thrills you? What are you passionate about? What fills you up? What do you love? Think it, do it, be it.

Journaling
Reflections on the Daily Inspiration

_____
_____
_____
_____
_____
_____
_____

August 30

What are you not accepting? Whatever you are not accepting causes your foot to be on the brake-pedal of your life. A lack of acceptance causes pain and stress. Today, attempt to accept things as they are.

Journaling
Reflections on the Daily Inspiration

___
___
___
___
___
___
___

August 31

What can we control? We can control how we treat ourselves and others. We can control our own intent to be loving or unloving, open or closed, protected or learning. What can't we control? We can't control others' feelings, behavior, and the outcome of things. Today, notice what you do have control over and what you only have influence over.

Journaling
Reflections on the Daily Inspiration

_____
_____
_____
_____
_____
_____
_____

September 1

Do you feel free to be who you are? If not, why not? Who or what are you allowing to limit your freedom to be yourself? No one but you can give you your inner freedom.

Journaling
Reflections on the Daily Inspiration

_____
_____
_____
_____
_____
_____
_____

September 2

What is your highest priority—having control over being safe, or being loving to yourself? The wounded self believes that trying to be safe is loving, but the resulting anxiety of trying to be safe lets you know that it is anything but loving. Today, notice your intent each moment—to be safe or to be loving to yourself.

Journaling
Reflections on the Daily Inspiration

_____
_____
_____
_____
_____
_____
_____

September 3

The spiritual journey is about letting go of the many layers of control. The less we try to control our pain, others, and outcomes, the more we will be in surrender to spirit's will for us and know our oneness with God. Today, compassionately, without judgment, notice your intent to control and gently open to learning with spirit about loving yourself and others.

Journaling
Reflections on the Daily Inspiration

September 4

What are you resisting? Are you resisting being controlled by yourself, by another, by spirit? Look at where you are stuck and notice what you may be resisting. Are you resisting taking loving action for yourself? Does taking loving action bring up an old loneliness of having to take care of yourself? The way out of resistance is to decide that loving yourself is more important than not being controlled or avoiding loneliness. Today, notice your resistance.

Journaling
Reflections on the Daily Inspiration

_____
_____
_____
_____
_____
_____
_____

September 5

Pain and joy are in the same place in the heart. You cannot put a lid on pain without putting a lid on your joy as well. Are you opting for the flatness of safety, or are you willing to experience both the lows and the highs of life? Today, cry and laugh with your whole heart.

Journaling
Reflections on the Daily Inspiration

_____
_____
_____
_____
_____
_____
_____

September 6

Do not pass up the opportunity to learn more about yourself when you find yourself with someone whom you judge. Your judgments of others are often a reflection of what you deny and judge in yourself. By taking the time to get to know someone whom you judge, you will find yourself knowing yourself better, and perhaps healing the judgments you have on yourself.

Journaling
Reflections on the Daily Inspiration

___
___
___
___
___
___
___

September 7

Guilt is often another way to avoid personal responsibility. As long as you feel guilty, you can beat yourself up for your choices, instead of using the same energy to make new, loving choices. Shame can also be another way of avoiding personal responsibility. As long as you tell yourself that you are not good enough, you don't have to learn to take loving care of yourself. When you open to truth and take loving actions for yourself and with others, you will no longer feel guilt and shame.

Journaling
Reflections on the Daily Inspiration

_____
_____
_____
_____
_____
_____

September 8

If you shut down your feelings to avoid pain, how can you ever know what is right or wrong for you? Spirit often speaks through your feelings, so when you are in the intent to protect against pain rather than in the intent to learn about love, you are shutting out the very guidance that you need to feel safe.

Journaling
Reflections on the Daily Inspiration

_____
_____
_____
_____
_____
_____

September 9

Grace is a gift of spirit that comes when we stay open to learning about loving ourselves and others. Grace is the feeling of extraordinary well-being that enters the heart when the heart is truly open. Grace is what we experience when love rather than fear is motivating our thoughts and behavior.

Journaling
Reflections on the Daily Inspiration

September 10

Are you trying to get love or share love? You can share love only if you have love to share, which is the case only when you are connecting with spirit and loving yourself. Loving yourself is not selfish—it is self-responsible. Today, focus on loving your inner child, rather than on getting love or approval.

Journaling
Reflections on the Daily Inspiration

_____
_____
_____
_____
_____
_____

September 11

Do you remember laughing with your whole body as a child? How often do you allow yourself to let go and laugh with your whole body as an adult? Joyous laughter is a balm for the soul. Laughter opens us to the experience of spirit. Today, let yourself laugh with your whole body and soul.

Journaling
Reflections on the Daily Inspiration

_____
_____
_____
_____
_____
_____

September 12

Embrace your tears of joy and gratitude for the beauty that surrounds us. Embrace your tears of sorrow for the loneliness and pain in our world. Your tears of joy and sorrow indicate that your heart is open. If you cannot weep in joy and sorrow, you cannot truly love.

Journaling
Reflections on the Daily Inspiration

___
___
___
___
___
___

September 13

When you reach all of your goals and are still not peaceful and fulfilled, consider that you may be creating inner emptiness because your goal is to get love, safety, security, and approval, rather than give love to yourself and others. Only when the love-that-is God is guiding your way, will your emptiness be filled.

Journaling
Reflections on the Daily Inspiration

_____
_____
_____
_____
_____
_____
_____

September 14

You will know that you are taking loving actions on your own behalf when the action feels right in your gut, right like a piece of a puzzle fitting into the right space. Notice these feelings of rightness in your being when you are taking loving action, as well as the feeling of tension when the action is not in your highest good. This is one of the ways spirit is always guiding you.

Journaling
Reflections on the Daily Inspiration

_____
_____
_____
_____
_____
_____
_____

September 15

Today, notice your wounded self with curiosity and a light heart. Move beyond judgment and into compassion for this sacred journey toward wholeness. It doesn't matter how far you are on this path—it only matters how you journey.

Journaling
Reflections on the Daily Inspiration

_____
_____
_____
_____
_____
_____
_____

September 16

Today, make sure you are regenerating your energy. Spend time in nature. Do something creative. Give love to someone who receives it lovingly. Receive love from someone who gives it lovingly. Laugh with someone. Play with someone. Play with an animal. Connect with spirit. Make sure your energy is getting recharged rather than depleted.

Journaling
Reflections on the Daily Inspiration

___
___
___
___
___
___

September 17

What are the characteristics you notice in yourself and others? Do you generally notice what is wrong or what is wonderful? Today notice your judgmental thoughts and replace them with kind, compassionate thoughts.

Journaling
Reflections on the Daily Inspiration

_____
_____
_____
_____
_____
_____
_____

September 18

Let us not deny or judge the wounded part of us that wants control over the outcome of things and believes we can have this control. Let us consciously choose to control, without judgment, instead of doing it unconsciously. By making it conscious and choosing it, the choice to love ourselves instead of trying to control others becomes available to us.

Journaling
Reflections on the Daily Inspiration

September 19

Do not give up on your dreams. Keep moving yourself forward, bit by bit, and you will get there, just as the tiny drops of water on a stone eventually wear down the stone. Spirit supports your highest good when you know what you want and are willing to take the necessary actions on your own behalf.

Journaling
Reflections on the Daily Inspiration

_____
_____
_____
_____
_____
_____
_____

September 20

You have within you the power to create a life of pain or a life of joy. If you follow the beliefs you were given, you will likely create a life of pain. If you follow the truth from spirit, you can create a life of joy. Today, allow the truth from spirit to guide you and notice how you feel.

Journaling
Reflections on the Daily Inspiration

September 21

Allow yourself to know what you know. Knowing is a direct experience of spirit. What we think we know when we think, are thoughts we make up—our own beliefs. Knowing is a solid feeling of being in truth and comes directly from spirit.

Journaling
Reflections on the Daily Inspiration

_____
_____
_____
_____
_____
_____
_____

September 22

Let your first thought when you awaken be of gratitude. Thank God for keeping your soul safe in the night. Thank God for the sacred privilege of being in a body and having the opportunity to evolve your soul in love. Thank God for whatever you have that is meaningful to you. And let the last thought you have before you go to sleep be of gratitude.

Journaling
Reflections on the Daily Inspiration

_____
_____
_____
_____
_____
_____
_____

September 23

Today, notice, without judgment, the various ways you try to control others and outcomes. Do you get angry, blame, give yourself up, resist, worry, and ruminate? Do these choices actually give you control, or do they just make you feel anxious? Noticing without judgment can give you new choices.

Journaling
Reflections on the Daily Inspiration

September 24

Fun and joy exist between two people when the energy is clear and flowing between them. Clear energy is the result of open, spiritually connected hearts. Likewise, intimacy and passion in committed relationships are the result of clear, heart-centered energy. The words "I love you" mean nothing without the clear spiritual energy of the open heart.

Journaling
Reflections on the Daily Inspiration

September 25

If someone's behavior makes your stomach tight, attend. Your stomach may be reacting to an energy that is unloving. It is only when you attend to your inner feelings that you can take loving action on your own behalf.

Journaling
Reflections on the Daily Inspiration

_____
_____
_____
_____
_____
_____
_____

September 26

What can you do today to make a difference in someone's life? You can offer a kind word, a warm smile, a loving touch, loving laughter, appreciation and acknowledgment, a listening ear, emotional support, physical help, your time and attention. Today, think about what you can do to make a difference in someone's life.

Journaling
Reflections on the Daily Inspiration

_____
_____
_____
_____
_____
_____

September 27

Is the fear of failure or of success keeping you immobilized? Do you fear rejection if you fail? Do you fear demands and expectations if you succeed? Until you are ready to manage rejection without it defining your worth and set loving limits regarding demands and expectations, you may stay stuck in procrastination. Only you, operating as a spiritually connected loving adult, can manage rejection and demands. Today, practice being a loving adult.

Journaling
Reflections on the Daily Inspiration

September 28

Which will be your guide today, fear or love? Which will light your way today, your desire to control or your desire to learn about love? If you do not consciously think about it, fear and the desire to control will be in charge. The intent to control is the automatic, unconscious, default setting of your internal computer. Today choose to be conscious of who is in charge, your wounded self, or your loving adult.

Journaling
Reflections on the Daily Inspiration

_____
_____
_____
_____
_____
_____

September 29

Do you feel alone? Are you having problems with your spiritual connection? The intent to control others cuts off your connection with your guidance. So does the intent to control your feelings with too much food, junk food, alcohol, and drugs. Today, notice your intent.

Journaling
Reflections on the Daily Inspiration

_____
_____
_____
_____
_____
_____
_____

September 30

Today, practice being fully present in this moment. Instead of focusing on doing, allow your doing to come from your being. Notice the beauty around you—people, animals, flowers, trees, the sky and clouds, colors, art. Allow yourself to feel the joy of beauty within your being.

Journaling
Reflections on the Daily Inspiration

October 1

When fear and anxiety well up within, it is an opportunity to open to learning about what you are telling yourself and how you are treating yourself that's causing these feelings. Then explore your false beliefs and turn to your guidance for the truth and loving action. Choosing to be in the present moment with the power of love will move you beyond the fear that comes from your wounded self.

Journaling
Reflections on the Daily Inspiration

_____
_____
_____
_____
_____
_____
_____

October 2

Are you a good friend? Do you keep in contact with your friends? Are you there for your friends when they need you? Today, be the kind of friend that you would like others to be with you.

Journaling
Reflections on the Daily Inspiration

___
___
___
___
___
___
___

October 3

What do you do in conflict? Do you learn or do you run? Do you use conflict as an opportunity to evolve your soul in love, or do you do all you can to avoid the conflict or control the outcome? We learn through adversity. Today, embrace conflict as a wonderful opportunity to learn.

Journaling
Reflections on the Daily Inspiration

October 4

Your essence is beauty. Your essence is joy. Your essence is peace, love, creativity, passion. Your essence is a perfect and individualized expression of spirit. Today, and each day, choose to be a loving guardian of your sacred self.

Journaling
Reflections on the Daily Inspiration

October 5

Dogs are always happy to see us, even if we have been gone only five minutes. Dogs forgive us instantly, even if we scare them. Dogs are sensitive to our feelings and care about our well-being. Dogs love us unconditionally, even when we are not being loving. Dogs can be our teachers if we allow them to be.

Journaling
Reflections on the Daily Inspiration

October 6

Today, notice whether or not you WANT responsibility for your feelings rather than for others' feelings. You can want this only from your loving adult, not from your wounded self, who wants to control others by taking responsibility for their feelings and making them responsible for yours.

Journaling
Reflections on the Daily Inspiration

October 7

When you move into this moment with gratitude and appreciation, you open your heart and invite in the presence of spirit. This week, practice remembering gratitude and appreciation and notice the aliveness of spirit within you.

Journaling
Reflections on the Daily Inspiration

October 8

When something good happens for another, do you feel jealous or happy for them? Do you support them or tear them down? If you find yourself being jealous and unsupportive, explore how you may not be supporting yourself in being all you can be.

Journaling
Reflections on the Daily Inspiration

October 9

Speak your truth to others in the moment. If you choose not to speak your truth in the moment, then wait until you are both open to learning. Resenting the other when you choose not to speak your truth and not to open to learning only leads to stress and distance with others.

Journaling
Reflections on the Daily Inspiration

October 10

The avoidance of feeling loneliness and heartbreak is often at the root of controlling, compliant, resistant, or addictive behavior. It is helpful to learn to name the feeling we are trying to avoid. When we name it, we can allow it, acknowledge it, embrace it, bring love to it, and then release it to spirit. Denying it keeps us stuck. Naming it allows us to manage it, release it, and take loving action to relieve it.

Journaling
Reflections on the Daily Inspiration

October 11

Gratitude for everyday experiences is a doorway to peace and joy. Thanking God for the beauty of a flower, for the hot water that comes from the faucet, for a warm bed and food to eat, for caring and friendship, for rain and sunshine and the myriad of other everyday experiences can bring great joy to the heart.

Journaling
Reflections on the Daily Inspiration

_____
_____
_____
_____
_____
_____

October 12

Are you hanging on to the past as a way to not be responsible for the present? Are you blaming your present on your past? If you are, then you are still operating from the beliefs you concluded long ago. Opening to exploring your limiting beliefs in the present, and bringing in the truth from your guidance, will help you to release the past and be fully present to manifest the gifts of your true soul self.

Journaling
Reflections on the Daily Inspiration

October 13

Today, think about softness—the softness of your smile, of your kindness and caring, of the tenderness of your touch. There is such power in softness. Today, discern the difference between softness and weakness. Weakness is allowing others to run over you and control you. Softness is the result of a powerful loving adult standing in your truth and being unafraid to express your love.

Journaling
Reflections on the Daily Inspiration

October 14

Think of your individual mind as an individual computer, with its limited information. Think of the greater mind, the mind of spirit, as having all the information there is. Who is more capable of being in charge of your life—your individual mind or the great mind? Why not put yourself in the care of your higher self rather than your wounded self?

Journaling
Reflections on the Daily Inspiration

_____
_____
_____
_____
_____
_____

October 15

Are you kind to yourself or judgmental toward yourself? Your kindness toward others will always be subverted by your angry inner child when you indulge your wounded self in judging yourself. Judgment toward others is the natural result of self-judgment. Today, notice your self-judgments and choose kindness toward yourself.

Journaling
Reflections on the Daily Inspiration

October 16

Today, notice all self-judgment as a form of control. "If I judge myself, then others won't judge me." If I judge myself, I can get myself to perform, to accomplish, to do it right" "If I judge myself as being flawed and therefore the cause of others' rejecting behavior, I can continue the illusion that I cause others' feelings and behavior." Today, notice your false beliefs about judgment and control.

Journaling
Reflections on the Daily Inspiration

___
___
___
___
___
___

October 17

We do not heal alone. We all need the caring, support, and honest reflection of others to know ourselves and move beyond the false beliefs that limit us. The wounded self may falsely believe that we have to handle our challenges alone, that we are weak if we need help, but the loving adult takes the loving action of reaching out to others for the necessary help.

Journaling
Reflections on the Daily Inspiration

___
___
___
___
___
___

October 18

You will feel alive when your intent is to love yourself and others. You will feel flat when your intent is to have control over getting love and avoiding pain. Your intent can change from moment to moment, and your feelings change with your intent. Today, notice your feelings, then notice your intent.

Journaling
Reflections on the Daily Inspiration

___
___
___
___
___
___

October 19

Joy and love are what we feel when we have surrendered to spirit guiding our life. Fear is what we feel when our ego wounded self is in charge. Yet our wounded self fears the surrender, fearing loss of self. We need to be willing to heal the false self to gain the true self.

Journaling
Reflections on the Daily Inspiration

_____
_____
_____
_____
_____
_____

October 20

Most of our judgments of others are projections of our own inner upsets and self-judgments. Notice your judgments toward others. How are they projections of you own inner insecurities and fears?

Journaling
Reflections on the Daily Inspiration

___
___
___
___
___
___
___

October 21

Are there people in your life towards whom you hold a grudge? Resentment is a low frequency, so letting go of it in your heart lightens you. You don't need to see this person if it is not in your highest good to do so, but letting go of resentment is always in your highest good.

Journaling
Reflections on the Daily Inspiration

_____
_____
_____
_____
_____
_____
_____

October 22

Today, notice what you do when pain comes up—especially the pain of loneliness and heartache when someone is rejecting or controlling with you. Do you get irritated, angry, or judgmental? Do you resist or withdraw? Do you people-please and give yourself up? Do you numb out with food or other substances, or with activities such as TV or the Internet? Notice the ways you avoid the pain of loneliness and heartache.

Journaling
Reflections on the Daily Inspiration

___
___
___
___
___
___

October 23

Focus on the physical sensations in your gut today. What emotions do you associate with these sensations? What are you thinking to cause these emotions? Ask spirit what thoughts would create joy today.

Journaling
Reflections on the Daily Inspiration

October 24

You will experience freedom when you no longer fear being rejected or controlled by others. When you define yourself through spirit and are guided by spirit toward your own highest good, you will move beyond the fears of rejection and engulfment and into the freedom to be all that you are.

Journaling
Reflections on the Daily Inspiration

October 25

It is not what we do or what we say in a moment that defines us in that moment, but rather the energy with which we speak and act. Our energy in any given moment is open or closed, loving or unloving, accepting or judgmental, kind or unkind, soft or hard, flexible or unyielding, controlling or learning. Regardless of the words, the energy always betrays our intent.

Journaling
Reflections on the Daily Inspiration

October 26

Joy, fun and passion with another are the results of connection. Connection is the result of two people coming together with open hearts. An open heart is the result of choosing to make loving yourself and others your highest priority, more important than getting love, avoiding pain, or being safe from rejection or engulfment.

Journaling
Reflections on the Daily Inspiration

___
___
___
___
___
___

October 27

Who or what do you blame for your anger, hurt, anxiety, depression? Do you blame a person? Do you blame God? Do you blame circumstances? Blaming outside yourself is one of the causes of your unhappiness—it keeps you trapped. Look to your own thoughts and behavior. If you are not being kind to yourself and others in thoughts and actions, you will be unhappy. Happiness is an inside job, resulting from your intent to learn and love.

Journaling
Reflections on the Daily Inspiration

___
___
___
___
___
___

October 28

Notice your anger, frustration, or irritation. These feelings are always an indication that you are not taking care of yourself in some way. Your inner child is angry at you for the lack of care and may be projecting it outside yourself to others. Attend to your anger and discover what loving actions you need to take on your own behalf.

Journaling
Reflections on the Daily Inspiration

___
___
___
___
___

October 29

Today, focus on telling your truth with each person you meet—the truth about you and who you are, not about them and who they are. Notice when you want to change the truth, or to withhold something. Notice the fear of being completely and radically honest with your truth about who you are. What is your fear?

Journaling
Reflections on the Daily Inspiration

October 30

Feeling great? Enjoy it! Feeling upset, scared, depressed, anxious, angry? Learn from it! Enjoy the up times, learn from the down times. Each time you learn from the down times, the up times bring more and more joy. In the up times, do not think you are "there"—the down times will come. In the down times, do not think they will last forever, the up times will come.

Journaling
Reflections on the Daily Inspiration

___
___
___
___
___
___

October 31

It is challenging to experience our lack of control over others and outcomes. Yet peace of mind lies in this acceptance. When you accept your powerlessness over others, then you can turn your attention to what you do have control over—your own thoughts and behavior and create the inner peace and joy that only you can create.

Journaling
Reflections on the Daily Inspiration

_____
_____
_____
_____
_____
_____

November 1

Which journey do you focus on—the earthly journey or the soul's journey? When focused on the earthly journey, we want to get all we can while attempting to control others and outcomes. When focused on the soul's journey, we surrender to our spiritual guidance, allowing the love that is God to guide us. We are here to evolve our souls in love. Today, focus on the spiritual journey of the soul.

Journaling
Reflections on the Daily Inspiration

November 2

Do not expect to ever find a time or place where there is no darkness. The darkness is here to challenge us to be in the light. This is why we came to this planet—to define who we are when darkness comes our way. Without darkness, there is no challenge to be in the light. Instead of joining the darkness by going into anger or fear, challenge yourself to stay in the light regardless of the circumstances.

Journaling
Reflections on the Daily Inspiration

_____
_____
_____
_____
_____
_____
_____

November 3

Focus today on kindness and caring for yourself and others. Focus on feeling your compassion for your own feelings and for the feelings of others. Caring for others without caring for yourself is manipulative. Caring just about yourself and ignoring the feelings of others is self-centered. Caring about yourself and others is loving.

Journaling
Reflections on the Daily Inspiration

_____
_____
_____
_____
_____
_____
_____

November 4

The heart rejoices when you are in the moment—letting go of past judgments of yourself and others, letting go of past hurts, letting go of regrets, letting go of worry about the future. The heart fills with the love that is God when you are fully in the moment. Today, challenge yourself to be present and mindful, moment-by-moment.

Journaling
Reflections on the Daily Inspiration

_____
_____
_____
_____
_____
_____
_____

November 5

Do you think more about what you have or about what you don't have? Notice the warmth and peace you feel when you are grateful for what you have. Notice the anxiety and sadness you feel when you think about what you don't have. Today, consciously choose gratitude throughout the day for every blessing that comes your way.

Journaling
Reflections on the Daily Inspiration

_____
_____
_____
_____
_____
_____
_____

November 6

Which is easier for you to offer—appreciation and understanding, or judgment? Today, make a decision to allow no judgment and focus on giving appreciation and understanding to yourself and others.

Journaling
Reflections on the Daily Inspiration

November 7

Notice where your thoughts are right now. Are they in the past? Are they in the future? Bring them into this present moment. Notice your breath, your life force, your feelings. Notice the beauty of nature or an object of beauty around you and let love for beauty fill your heart. Feel gratitude for the sacred privilege of your life.

Journaling
Reflections on the Daily Inspiration

_____
_____
_____
_____
_____
_____
_____

November 8

Keep the vision in your mind of what brings you joy. Let the vision of your joy guide you. Let the feeling of joy enliven and sustain you. Your feeling of joy is an invitation to spirit to support the manifestation of that which brings you joy.

Journaling
Reflections on the Daily Inspiration

___
___
___
___
___
___
___

November 9

Is there anyone on the planet who can actually take better care of your feelings than you? No one but you can be immediately aware of what you feel and need. Instead of making others responsible for your feelings—for your inner child—decide today to adopt your inner child and learn how, with your spiritual guidance, to take loving care of yourself.

Journaling
Reflections on the Daily Inspiration

___
___
___
___
___
___

November 10

Have you ever noticed that when you smile you feel good? Or do you believe that you have to feel good first to smile? Try smiling more and notice how you feel!

Journaling
Reflections on the Daily Inspiration

___
___
___
___
___
___
___

November 11

Laughter raises the frequency and is healing for the soul. Our essence takes life lightly and finds humor even in difficult times. Our wounded self often wants to take things very seriously. Today, choose lightness of being and allow the laughter to flow.

Journaling
Reflections on the Daily Inspiration

_____
_____
_____
_____
_____
_____

November 12

Our addictions—to busyness, substances, activities—cover up our fear of loneliness, heartbreak, and helplessness over others. Yet, when we are willing to feel these feelings with compassion for ourselves, they move through, and we are lighter. Today, take time to compassionately feel the feelings you are trying to avoid with your addictions.

Journaling
Reflections on the Daily Inspiration

_____
_____
_____
_____
_____
_____
_____

November 13

One of the big challenges of life is to stay in the moment. Notice how often your thoughts are on the past or future. How often are you fully in this moment, fully feeling your experience of this moment? The past is gone, and the future doesn't exist. Life is about the fullness of this moment.

Journaling
Reflections on the Daily Inspiration

November 14

There are two ways of knowing things. One is the intellectual way—through books, TV, the Internet, and other forms of external learning. The other is direct—opening to spirit and accessing truth. It is of great benefit when learning externally to always check in and see if what you are reading or hearing is truth.

Journaling
Reflections on the Daily Inspiration

_____
_____
_____
_____
_____
_____

November 15

Let your doing be an expression of your being, rather than a definition of your being. If you let go of the outcome of any endeavor, and allow the process to joyfully unfold, then there is no failure. Failure is a concept attached to outcomes, not to process.

Journaling
Reflections on the Daily Inspiration

_____
_____
_____
_____
_____
_____
_____

November 16

What do you do when you are scared or hurt? Do you get angry, withdraw, resist, or give yourself up? Do you explain, defend, go numb or get busy? Do you blame or punish others for your feelings? Today, focus on staying open and loving in the face of fear or hurt, and ask spirit for help in discovering the loving action.

Journaling
Reflections on the Daily Inspiration

_____
_____
_____
_____
_____
_____

November 17

Spiritual growth is like the perennial flowers that emerge, bloom, die, and then come back again next year, fuller and more beautiful. When we open to learning, evolution and change will always occur, and the deaths of our false beliefs open the way to the emergence of the beauty and fullness of our true selves.

Journaling
Reflections on the Daily Inspiration

_____
_____
_____
_____
_____
_____
_____

November 18

Whenever you feel down or anxious, it is likely that your wounded self is in charge, trying to control something and avoid something. How are you not taking care of yourself? What are you thinking or doing that is not in your highest good? Put your loving adult in charge—with an intent to learn and a connection to spirit—and you will instantly feel lighter and more peaceful.

Journaling
Reflections on the Daily Inspiration

November 19

Do you believe that if you punish others with anger and withdrawal they will change and be the way you want them to be? They may sometimes do what you want to avoid your anger or withdrawal, but they will not love you more—you cannot control their love. They may also become angry and withdrawn and then the connection is gone. Today, remember why you love them.

Journaling
Reflections on the Daily Inspiration

November 20

Imagination is a great gift—a doorway to spirit. Let yourself imagine, let yourself dream. All form starts with the imagination. The only caution regards your intent: Are you imagining from your essence to move toward full manifestation of self? Even with your imagination, be aware of your intent.

Journaling
Reflections on the Daily Inspiration

_____
_____
_____
_____
_____
_____

November 21

What is your first reaction when someone is harsh, critical, sarcastic, angry, judgmental, attacking? Do you attack back? Do you withdraw and get silent? Do you defend and explain? Today, honor the feeling in your body that says, "This doesn't feel good" and speak your truth without blame, defense, or judgment.

Journaling
Reflections on the Daily Inspiration

_____
_____
_____
_____
_____
_____

November 22

Do you have a belief that you will finally "get there?" Believing that you will get there, and then not ever getting there can feel discouraging. Instead of trying to reach some fantasy state of being, accept that life is an endless process of evolution. Life is about who you choose to be each moment rather than about getting somewhere. You are already "there" whenever you choose to be a caring and compassionate person.

Journaling
Reflections on the Daily Inspiration

___
___
___
___
___
___

November 23

You cannot control another's caring about you. Others are either essentially caring or they are not, and it has nothing to do with you. Being caring is a soul quality of a person—who they essentially are and therefore cannot be turned on and off. It is a way of being in the world.

Journaling
Reflections on the Daily Inspiration

_____
_____
_____
_____
_____
_____

November 24

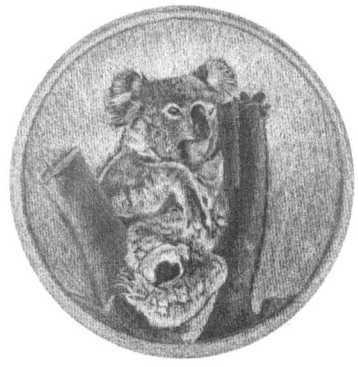

When there is peace within, take the time to open to your guidance. When there are no problems to explore, guidance comes forth with creative ideas that support your joy, passion, and purpose. Staying connected with guidance in the good times will bring great reward.

Journaling
Reflections on the Daily Inspiration

___
___
___
___
___
___

November 25

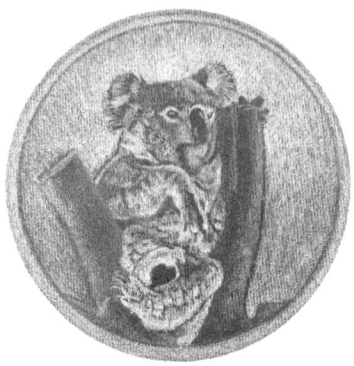

Information about you from another's wounded self is always about control rather than about love. It is not helpful to you, even if it is accurate. It is loving to you to let others know that you do not want information about yourself unless you ask for it. Ask for it only from people who have your highest good at heart, not from people who have an agenda for you. Ask for it from people who have a strong loving adult.

Journaling
Reflections on the Daily Inspiration

November 26

It is in your highest good and the highest good of all to be in reality regarding your intent and others' intent. You will not be able to make loving decisions on your own behalf if you are not in reality regarding another's intent. Your Inner child will be harmed if you believe that another is open to learning and devoted to caring when the other is really closed and self-absorbed. Today, choose to discern who is caring and who is not.

Journaling
Reflections on the Daily Inspiration

_____
_____
_____
_____
_____
_____

November 27

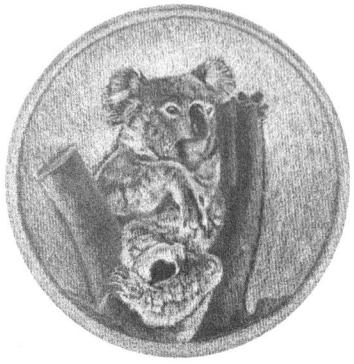

It is easy for most of us to judge ourselves and challenging to be compassionate toward ourselves. Yet it is compassion that motivates and heals. Today, notice your inner qualities—your caring, your goodness—and begin to connect these with your sense of worth.

Journaling
Reflections on the Daily Inspiration

November 28

Is there something you have always wanted to do but have not yet done? Is there something that would be fun, creative, and fulfilling that you keep putting off doing? Take a moment to look inside and discover what you might be passionate about that you are not paying attention to, and then notice what is in the way of taking this loving action. Today, begin to take the loving action.

Journaling
Reflections on the Daily Inspiration

November 29

What thoughts trigger your fear or anxiety? Thoughts of others' anger, rejection, withdrawal, smothering, demanding, questioning? Thoughts of work, of failure, of money, of time? The moment you notice a thought that is creating your fear, anxiety, or depression, counter the thought with a brief prayer—for peace, for love, for grace, for freedom.

Journaling
Reflections on the Daily Inspiration

_____
_____
_____
_____
_____
_____
_____

November 30

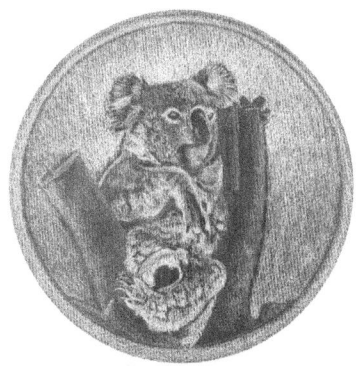

Notice if your focus is on caretaking others or taking care of yourself. Does your compassion go first to others, or first to your own feelings, your own inner child? Only when you have compassion for yourself first will you be able to take loving care of yourself and then extend your love and compassion to others. Compassion for others without caring for yourself may be manipulative—giving to get others to take care of you.

Journaling
Reflections on the Daily Inspiration

_____
_____
_____
_____
_____
_____
_____

December 1

Notice whether punishing others works to control them. When you get angry, judgmental, or withdrawn to control others, what actually happens? How do you end up feeling when you try to control others?

Journaling
Reflections on the Daily Inspiration

___
___
___
___
___
___
___

December 2

The desert fathers knew that if they could cry, they could open their hearts to God. Let yourself cry when your heart is moved. Authentic sadness opens the door to love and joy. If you put a lid on your tears, you also put a lid on your joy and ability to love. Today, let yourself cry when you heart is touched.

Journaling
Reflections on the Daily Inspiration

_____
_____
_____
_____
_____
_____

December 3

When someone who truly cares about you is angry at you, you can learn much by getting beyond the anger to what this person is really saying to you. When someone who loves you is angry with you, there is often a kernel of truth in what he or she is saying to you. Open your heart and hear, even in the face of anger.

Journaling
Reflections on the Daily Inspiration

December 4

Every relationship in our lives offers us a gift of growth. Think about your most difficult relationships—partner, family, friends, co-workers. Today, pick one to focus on. How is this person a mirror for you? How do you not take care of yourself around this person? What do you want from this person that you are not giving to yourself?

Journaling
Reflections on the Daily Inspiration

December 5

Remember throughout this day that you are on a spiritual journey to evolve your soul in love. Today, remember that you have the option to embrace each moment as an opportunity to learn about what is loving to you and others. Today, embrace all adversity as an opportunity to learn.

Journaling
Reflections on the Daily Inspiration

___
___
___
___
___
___

December 6

Today, attend to what you want. Listen to the inner promptings of your soul and spirit. Listen for what is loving to you—and then do it.

Journaling
Reflections on the Daily Inspiration

December 7

Who defines your worth? Do you give others the authority to decide if you are worthy, or unworthy, okay or not okay, adequate or inadequate? Does others' approval or disapproval define your worth and lovability? Today, give authority only to your spiritual guidance to define who you are.

Journaling
Reflections on the Daily Inspiration

_____
_____
_____
_____
_____
_____
_____

December 8

When you choose to be present with spirit, feeling the life force flowing through you, feeling the love-that-is-God that is you, then any task, no matter how mundane, is filled with the peace and joy of spirit. Your feelings are determined by who you choose to be, not by what you are doing.

Journaling
Reflections on the Daily Inspiration

___
___
___
___
___
___
___

December 9

Welcome conflict as an opportunity to challenge yourself to learn what spirit is trying to teach you about love. If you embrace conflict with a deep desire to learn rather that an intent to protect against that which you fear, you will discover the gems within the conflict.

Journaling
Reflections on the Daily Inspiration

_____
_____
_____
_____
_____
_____
_____

December 10

Everything has wisdom for you because everything is an expression of God. If you open to learning with the trees, the rocks, with the animals and with each other, you will learn about love and the soul's journey. When you ask your guidance questions and imagine the answers, you tap into the wisdom of the universe.

Journaling
Reflections on the Daily Inspiration

_____
_____
_____
_____
_____
_____

December 11

When someone behaves in a way that you don't like, you have only two choices: open to learning and reach full acceptance or accept that their behavior is not tolerable to you and leave. Trying to change them is not an option, for only they can change themselves, and only if they want to.

Journaling
Reflections on the Daily Inspiration

___
___
___
___
___
___
___

December 12

One of the best ways of feeling great is to speak up for yourself. If someone is mean, judgmental, sarcastic, speak up for yourself. Say, "That felt awful," or "Ouch," or " I don't want to be around you when you treat me like that," or "I know you're feeling badly, but I don't like it when take it out on me." Today, speak up for yourself.

Journaling
Reflections on the Daily Inspiration

_____
_____
_____
_____
_____
_____

December 13

Today, remember that you are a child of God. Remember that spirit supports your highest good at all times. Remember that it is your birthright to give and to receive. Remember that we live in an abundant universe and that you have a right to and are deserving of that abundance.

Journaling
Reflections on the Daily Inspiration

___
___
___
___
___
___
___

December 14

If you have given and given to others and have not received love in return, consider that you may be giving to get from an empty place within, rather than giving from an inner place that is overflowing with love. Turn your attention to filling your own emptiness first, and you will find yourself finally feeling loved.

Journaling
Reflections on the Daily Inspiration

_____
_____
_____
_____
_____
_____
_____

December 15

Today, notice if you are harming yourself with your thoughts—with your judgment and criticism, should and should not, right, wrong, good, bad. Today, remember that you always have good reasons for your feelings and behavior and explore rather than judge.

Journaling
Reflections on the Daily Inspiration

_____
_____
_____
_____
_____
_____
_____

December 16

Today, remember that your soul is forever, on its incredible journey of love. Gain comfort from knowing that only your body can die but that you, the individual expression of the Divine that is you, is forever. Knowing that you are forever is both a freedom and a responsibility.

Journaling
Reflections on the Daily Inspiration

_____
_____
_____
_____
_____
_____
_____

December 17

Take a moment right now and tune into your feelings, your inner child. Do you stand up for this child? Are you this child's advocate? Do you speak your truth for this child without attack, anger, or blame? Does your child feel safe within, knowing you are here as a loving adult? Today, practice speaking up for yourself without attacking, getting angry, or blaming anyone.

Journaling
Reflections on the Daily Inspiration

_____
_____
_____
_____
_____
_____
_____

December 18

Notice throughout this day what gives you energy and what drains your energy. Which people are givers, and which are takers? Which experiences energize and which are depleting? What thoughts fill you and what thoughts create emptiness? Become conscious of what gives to you and what takes from you.

Journaling
Reflections on the Daily Inspiration

December 19

Don't forget to "tune in" and "tune up"—checking in with your feelings and with your guidance throughout the day!

Journaling
Reflections on the Daily Inspiration

_____
_____
_____
_____
_____
_____
_____

December 20

If you are not feeling peaceful, attend to the thought that is limiting you. If you are not joyful, attend to the belief that is limiting you. If you are not feeling peace and joy, you are not being loving to yourself in some way. Today, become conscious of your thoughts and beliefs that are limiting you.

Journaling
Reflections on the Daily Inspiration

_____
_____
_____
_____
_____
_____
_____

December 21

Since we cannot know what the next moment will bring, why not be fully in this moment? When we spend our energy on the past and future, we miss the fullness of the now. Today, focus on your present inner experience.

Journaling
Reflections on the Daily Inspiration

___
___
___
___
___
___
___

December 22

The path of love is not the easy path—it is the road less traveled. It requires letting go of all power and control over others and outcomes. It requires strict adherence to truth and integrity, to living and speaking the radical truth. Today, be truthful with yourself about what path you are on—the path of fear, control, and avoidance of pain, or the path of courage, integrity, truth, and love.

Journaling
Reflections on the Daily Inspiration

_____
_____
_____
_____
_____
_____

December 23

Do you have the courage, honor, and integrity to tell your truth? (Not your opinion—your truth). Telling your truth is often challenging, but it is the only way your inner child will feel safe. You cannot feel safe within if you are lying to avoid confrontation. Inner safety is the result of having the courage to be an advocate for yourself.

Journaling
Reflections on the Daily Inspiration

___
___
___
___
___
___

December 24

Today, notice whether it is more important to you to be right or to be loving. The wounded self is devoted to being right. The loving adult is willing to let go of having to be right, and of having to win. Today, let the choice to be right or to be loving be a conscious choice.

Journaling
Reflections on the Daily Inspiration

December 25

Are you in resistance? Do you resist opening to learning? Do you resist opening to your spiritual guidance? Do you resist taking loving action for yourself? Do you resist loving others? Today embrace your resistance as if it is a fearful child or adolescent. Bringing love to the resistant part of yourself can move you out of staying stuck.

Journaling
Reflections on the Daily Inspiration

_____
_____
_____
_____
_____
_____
_____

December 26

Who makes your decisions—your wounded self or your loving adult? You might want to notice that decisions made from your wounded self rarely turn out well. You will always be guided toward your highest good when your loving adult is open to learning with spirit about what is truly loving to you.

Journaling
Reflections on the Daily Inspiration

_____
_____
_____
_____
_____
_____

December 27

Today, view people with your heart. Your mind cannot see who they really are. Only your heart can see who they are under their woundedness. Only your heart can see another's essential self, the true self. See others true selves with your heart and feel your own.

Journaling
Reflections on the Daily Inspiration

December 28

When we don't surrender to spirit, it is because we have hope of having control—over people, outcomes, and our own feelings. Today, notice how often your thoughts turn to, "If I do this, then this will happen." "If I say this, then the other person will react in this way." Our hope of control is very deep, but it will never bring us true peace and safety.

Journaling
Reflections on the Daily Inspiration

_____
_____
_____
_____
_____
_____

December 29

Seek not to give authority to others to tell you who you are or what is right or wrong for you. When you open to your spiritual guidance, you become the world's authority on you! Only your own guidance knows who you are and what is in your highest good. Today, seek to know yourself and support your highest good through inviting your guidance into your heart.

Journaling
Reflections on the Daily Inspiration

___
___
___
___
___
___

December 30

When we connect with spirit and fill ourselves with love, our love overflows and we want to share it with others. How do you want to share your love today? How do you want to show your caring? What service to others do you want to express today?

Journaling
Reflections on the Daily Inspiration

_____
_____
_____
_____
_____
_____

December 31

How often do you take good care of yourself until you are around another person with whom you are in relationship? How often do you drop the hand of your inner child as soon as you hope to get love from another? You will feel abandoned whenever you abandon yourself, and the other person will feel pulled on to fill you up. Today, practice staying conscious of your child—your feelings—all day.

Journaling
Reflections on the Daily Inspiration

_____
_____
_____
_____
_____
_____
_____

About the Author

DR. MARGARET PAUL is the cocreator of Inner Bonding®, along with Dr. Erika Chopich, and is author/coauthor of several best-selling books, including *Do I Have to Give Up Me to Be Loved by You?*; *Do I Have to Give Up Me to Be Loved By You?: The Workbook*; *Inner Bonding*; *Healing Your Aloneness*; *The Healing Your Aloneness Workbook*; *Do I Have to Give Up Me to Be Loved by My Kids?*; *Do I Have to Give Up Me to Be Loved by God?*; *Diet for Divine Connection: Beyond Junk Foods and Junk Thoughts to At-Will Spiritual Connection*; *The Inner Bonding Workbook: Six Steps to Healing Yourself and Connecting with Your Divine Guidance*, and *Six Steps to Total Self-Healing: The Inner Bonding Process*.

Dr. Paul's books have been distributed around the world and have been translated into many languages. She holds a PhD in psychology and is a relationship expert, noted public speaker, workshop leader, educator, consultant, and artist. She has appeared on many radio and TV shows, including *The Oprah Show*. She has successfully worked with tens of thousands of individuals, couples, and business relationships and has taught classes and seminars since 1967.

Margaret continues to work with individuals, couples, and groups throughout the world on the phone, Zoom, and Skype. During her sessions, workshops, and Intensives, she is able to access her own and her clients' spiritual guidance, which enables her to work with people wherever they are in the world. She offers life-changing thirty-day courses, and she continues to conduct One-Day Inner Bonding Breakthroughs, Inner Bonding Workshops and Three-Day and Five-Day Inner Bonding intensives. She continues to develop content for www.innerbonding.com, and her passion is distributing SelfQuest®, the online program that teaches Inner Bonding. It is being offered to prisons and schools and sold to the general public.

In her spare time, Margaret loves to paint, make pottery, read, learn, grow, and spend time with her loved ones.

www.ingramcontent.com/pod-product-compliance
Lightning Source LLC
Chambersburg PA
CBHW072146070526
44585CB00015B/1014